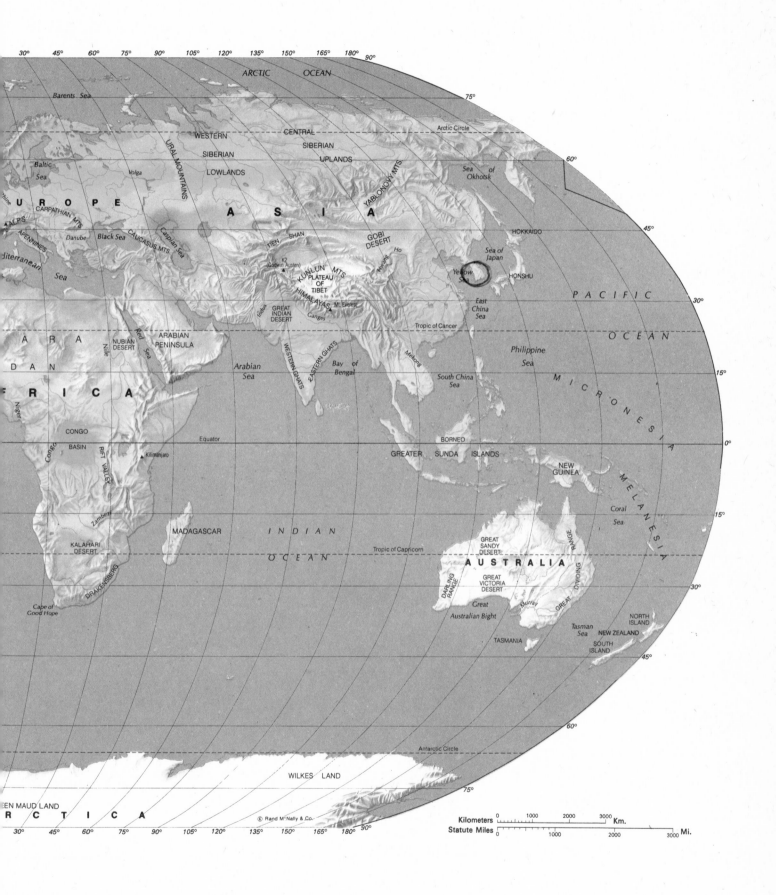

30° 45° 60° 75° 90° 105° 120° 135° 150° 165° 180° 90°

ARCTIC OCEAN

75°

Barents Sea

Arctic Circle

60°

WESTERN CENTRAL
SIBERIAN SIBERIAN
URAL MOUNTAINS LOWLANDS UPLANDS

Baltic
Sea
Volga

Sea of
Okhotsk

EUROPE

ASIA

45°

CARPATHIAN MTS

ALPS

Caspian Sea

YABLONOYI MTS

HOKKAIDO

APENNINES

Danube Black Sea CAUCASUS MTS

TIEN SHAN

GOBI
DESERT

Sea of
Japan

Mediterranean
Sea

K2
(Godwin Austen)

KUNLUN MTS

Hwang Ho

Yellow
Sea

HONSHU

PACIFIC

30°

PLATEAU
OF
TIBET

ARA

NUBIAN
DESERT

ARABIAN
PENINSULA

Red Sea

Nile

HIMALAYAS

Mt. Everest

East
China
Sea

OCEAN

DAN

Indus

GREAT
INDIAN
DESERT

Ganges

Tropic of Cancer

Arabian
Peninsula

WESTERN GHATS

EASTERN GHATS

Mekong

Philippine
Sea

15°

FRICA

Arabian
Sea

Bay
of
Bengal

South China
Sea

MICRONESIA

Niger

CONGO
BASIN

Equator

BORNEO

0°

RIFT VALLEY

Kilimanjaro

GREATER SUNDA ISLANDS

NEW
GUINEA

MELANESIA

Zambezi

MADAGASCAR

INDIAN

Coral
Sea

15°

KALAHARI
DESERT

OCEAN

Tropic of Capricorn

GREAT
SANDY
DESERT

GREAT DIVIDING RANGE

DRAKENSBERG

AUSTRALIA

Cape of
Good Hope

DARLING RANGE

GREAT
VICTORIA
DESERT

30°

Great
Australian Bight

Murray

NORTH
ISLAND

Tasman
Sea

NEW ZEALAND

TASMANIA

SOUTH
ISLAND

45°

60°

Antarctic Circle

75°

WILKES LAND

EN MAUD LAND

© Rand M⁓Nally & Co.

RCTICA

30° 45° 60° 75° 90° 105° 120° 135° 150° 165° 180° 90°

Kilometers 0 1000 2000 3000 Km.
Statute Miles 0 1000 2000 3000 Mi.

Children's Atlas of the World

Updated and Revised Edition

Rand McNally

Children's Atlas of the World

by Bruce Ogilvie, Ph.D.,
formerly, Lecturer, Department of Geography,
University of Chicago

and Douglas Waitley

Rand McNally & Company
Chicago • New York • San Francisco

Revised Edition, 1985

Library of Congress Cataloging in Publication Data

Ogilvie, Bruce
  Children's atlas of the world

  Includes index
  SUMMARY: Discusses such topics as the
formation and periodic changes of the earth's
surface, historical attempts to draw accurate
world maps, and the earth's various resources.
Also includes physical, political, cultural, and
faunal maps of six continents and a composite map
of Antarctica.
    1. Atlases.   2. Atlases—Juvenile literature.
[1. Atlases.   2. Maps]   I. Watley, Douglas.
II. Rand McNally and Company.   III. Title.
G1021.035   1979   912   79-13842
ISBN 0-528-82418-X

Fifth printing, 1985

Contents

Space Travelers

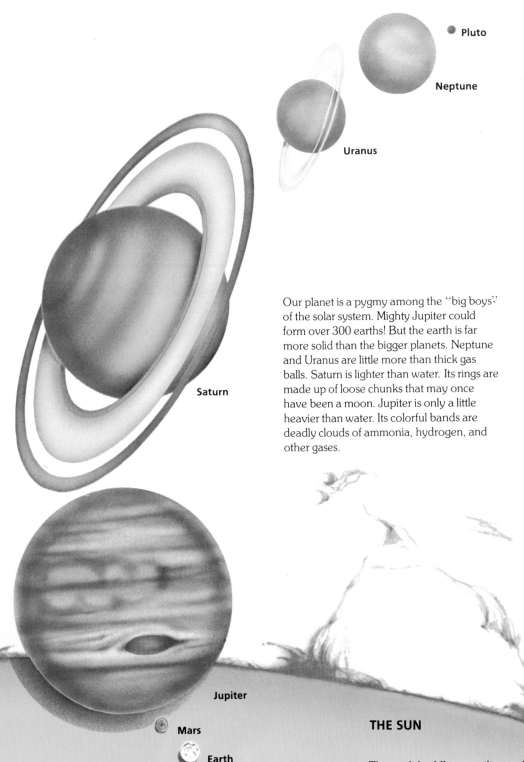

Pluto

Neptune

Uranus

Saturn

Our planet is a pygmy among the "big boys" of the solar system. Mighty Jupiter could form over 300 earths! But the earth is far more solid than the bigger planets. Neptune and Uranus are little more than thick gas balls. Saturn is lighter than water. Its rings are made up of loose chunks that may once have been a moon. Jupiter is only a little heavier than water. Its colorful bands are deadly clouds of ammonia, hydrogen, and other gases.

Jupiter

Mars

Earth

Moon

Venus

Mercury

THE SUN

The earth huddles near the sun for warmth. It is a delicate distance. A little closer and earth temperatures might reach the 900°F (482°C) of Venus. A shade farther out and they might dip to the −94°F (−70°C) of Mars. Beyond Mars the sun supplies little heat. The surface of Saturn is −285°F (−176°C). Seen from Pluto the sun is not much larger than any other star. The earth occupies the perfect location for life as we know it.

Hanging in the blackness of space like a glowing blue green oasis, the earth revolves quietly around the sun. The sun's gravitational pull keeps the earth from flinging itself into the starry reaches of outer space. But the earth, nevertheless, speeds on its circular course at the fantastic speed of 67,000 miles (107,823 kilometers) per hour —many times the rate of the fastest supersonic jet. After one year the earth has carried all of us on a rushing voyage of over 583 million miles (938,221,900 kilometers)!

As the earth sweeps onward, it is struck by energy rippling out from the sun at terrific speed. Part of this solar energy is visible to the human eye as light, which travels 186,282 miles (299,783 kilometers) in a single second. As the light waves smash into the earth, they create heat. The amount of heat created depends on the angle at which the sun's rays strike the earth. Summer and winter occur because of the tilt of the earth's axis. As the earth moves around the sun, this tilt never changes. It means that at times one of the poles is sunlit while the other is dark. It also means that sunlight at times strikes certain parts of the earth at more slanted angles, giving less warmth. Winter then occurs. It is all a matter of angles, not distance. For the earth is actually a little closer to the sun when January blizzards howl across Europe and North America than it is when the July thermometer pokes past 100°F (38°C).

In addition to its journey around the sun, the earth makes a rapid rotating movement on its axis. Once every twenty-four hours it turns completely around. As it does so, the sun seems to slip across the sky, rising in the east and setting in the west. But the sun is not moving. It is the earth whirling itself about like a merry-go-round that causes what seems to be the sun's motion.

Even ancient people were aware of the changes in the rising and setting of the sun. In winter the fiery globe seemed to rise in the southeast; in summer, in the northeast. Lands in the direction of the winter sunrise were said to be in the south, for the word *south* meant *sun* to the Indo-Europeans. Lands opposite the south were said to be *north,* which meant *beneath* the sun. *East* was the direction of the sunrise, and *west* was *away from* the sunrise.

The earth is accompanied around the sun by eight fellow planets. But none of these other planets can support life as we know it. Some, like Mercury and Venus, are sizzling hot. Others, like faraway Neptune and Pluto, are cold as tombstones. Most contain choking gases. Our planet is neither too close nor too far from the life-giving sun. The earth alone has scarlet flowers and swaying trees and creatures that laugh and cry and care for one another. It is the jewel of the solar system.

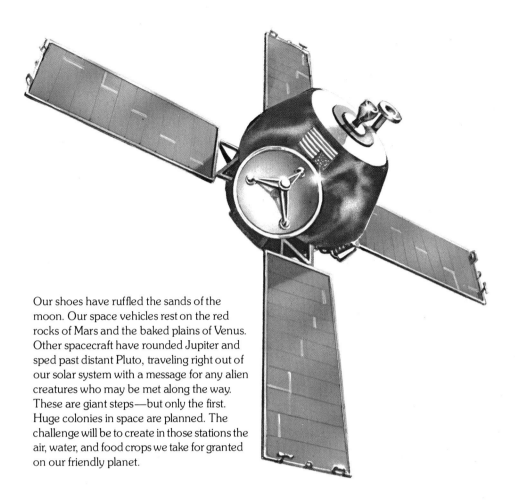

Our shoes have ruffled the sands of the moon. Our space vehicles rest on the red rocks of Mars and the baked plains of Venus. Other spacecraft have rounded Jupiter and sped past distant Pluto, traveling right out of our solar system with a message for any alien creatures who may be met along the way. These are giant steps—but only the first. Huge colonies in space are planned. The challenge will be to create in those stations the air, water, and food crops we take for granted on our friendly planet.

The earth makes a complete turn every twenty-four hours. This eastward movement is a help in launching spacecraft. A rocket shot eastward from Cape Canaveral gets a boost of nearly 900 miles (1,448.37 kilometers) per hour from the earth's spin.

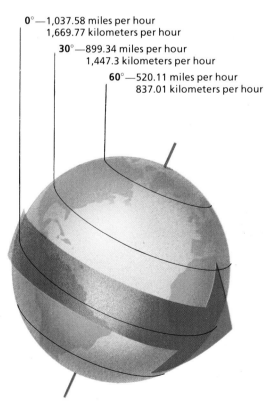

0°—1,037.58 miles per hour
1,669.77 kilometers per hour
30°—899.34 miles per hour
1,447.3 kilometers per hour
60°—520.11 miles per hour
837.01 kilometers per hour

The 23½° tilt of the earth's axis combined with the earth's yearly trip around the sun causes the seasons. During the northern hemisphere's summer the northern part of the earth is tipped toward the sun, receiving more heat. In spring and fall both parts of the globe receive equal amounts of sunlight. During its winter the northern part is tipped away from the sun and therefore receives less heat.

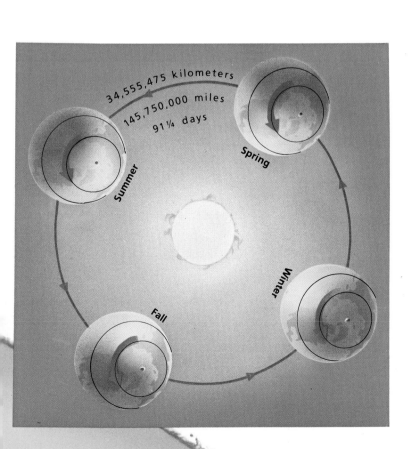

34,555,475 kilometers
145,750,000 miles
91¼ days

Summer

Spring

Winter

Fall

7

Forces That Shape the Earth

It is hard to realize that the Alps, the Andes, and the Rockies have not shoved their bony shoulders skyward forever. There was a time when the land they stand upon was level. At times the sea even covered this land and fishes darted over what would one day be a proud mountaintop.

There were no mountains when the earth began forming out of the gases and dust accompanying the birth of the sun. Gravitation pressed the materials into a tight knot that, from the pressure, became hotter than volcanic lava.

As the rocks melted, the lighter elements rose to the surface where they floated like tin pie plates on a kettle of soup. In a billion and a half years these "plates" cooled. Parts sank down to become the ocean basins and other parts formed the continents: Europe, North and South America, Africa, Asia, Australia, and Antarctica. The continents, however, were only flat chunks of land around twenty-five miles (40.23 kilometers) thick—paper thin compared to the 7,876 miles (12,713.4 kilometers) of the earth's white hot interior. Massive currents developed inside the earth and several thousand miles of melted rock began to churn like gigantic rivers of slow-moving lava beneath the surface. These currents brushed against the underparts of the continental plates. The continents were pushed at the rate of about two inches per year. In human terms this was very slow. But it meant that in just 10 million years a continental plate would move more than 300 miles (482.79 kilometers). It was only a matter of time before these drifting continents smacked into one another.

Around 400 million years ago North America and Europe met, closing the great prehistoric ocean that had separated them. As if on a conveyor belt, the rocks and sediments of this ocean floor were pushed together to form a section of the Appalachians and the mountains of Norway and Scotland. But this rise was not rapid. It took more than 100 million years to build these mountains. Europe and North America would again separate 85 million years later.

Great landmasses have been inching across the earth's surface for at least 600 million years. About 200 million years ago, the continents we know today fit together like a giant jigsaw puzzle. Scientists have given a name to that continent: Pangaea.

When Megalosaurus walked the earth 165 million years ago, the Atlantic was just beginning to form. Masses of melted rock pushed upward through a weak spot in the earth's crust, in time causing Europe and North America to split. Water drained off the land and filled the gap. The Atlantic Ocean was born.

Then, about 300 million years ago, Africa butted slowly into the North American-European plates. The result was the Harz Mountains in Germany, the Ardennes in Belgium, the Cornwall coast of England, and the hills of Ireland. These same mountain "ripples" also spread across what is now the eastern United States, for there was as yet no Atlantic Ocean to bar their way. This movement completed the Appalachian chain.

The great currents within the earth continued thrusting upward against the plates. Ever so slowly a break appeared between North America and Europe. Water drained off the land and began trickling into the gap. In ten thousand years a salty little bay a third of a mile (536.44 meters) wide developed between the drifting continents. In a million years the Atlantic Ocean was born.

As the North and South American plates inched westward, they began grinding over parts of the plate beneath the Pacific Ocean. The collision caused the Rockies and Andes to be forced slowly upward.

Shortly thereafter two other plate movements took place. Africa drifted northward against Europe, this time creating the Alps. And India pushed northward against Asia, forcing the once flat land to rise up to form the splendid Himalaya Mountains.

Even today the plates are moving. Mount Everest, the world's tallest mountain, is believed to be growing year by year. North America is rumbling over the Pacific plate, bringing earthquakes to California. The lands surrounding the Pacific are alive with volcanoes where one plate either moves over or sideswipes another. This explosive zone is well named "the Ring of Fire." The most spectacular of these towering volcanoes is Mauna Loa in Hawaii.

Hardly a place on earth has not felt an earth tremor in the recent past. Wherever these quakes occur, no matter how small they may be, plate movements are going on.

We are riding on a thin crust. Beneath us the force of nearly eight thousand miles (12,874.4 kilometers) of liquid rock is constantly reshaping the land upon which we live.

An erupting volcano is frightening proof of the enormous heat within the earth. Rock turned to liquid is called lava. Flowing lava chars and covers everything in its path.

From the beginning of time, people could only run from burning volcanic lava that buried their homes. Then, in 1973, villagers on the island of Heimaey, Iceland, fought back. Using huge pumps, they poured millions of tons of icy seawater over the approaching lava. Cooled to solid rock, the lava was stopped before it could entirely destroy the coastal town.

The Many Faces of Earth

The continents have a thousand ever-changing faces. There are craggy mountains broken by slow-moving glaciers. There are rugged coastlines where angry ocean waves splinter salt-splashed boulders. There are valleys echoing to great rivers that dig deeper as they carry rocks, sand, and pebbles toward a distant sea. There are shimmering deserts where hot whirlwinds hurl sands that scrape ancient rocks into fantastic mounds.

Snow and ice, rivers and oceans, sandstorms and whirlwinds—all constantly chisel away at the earth. Although these forces work slowly, in the long run not even the most massive granite range can withstand them. Once America's rounded Appalachians were probably higher than the Himalaya Mountains. The low Ore Mountains of Czechoslovakia are also worn-down remains of once lofty peaks formed several hundred million years ago.

The work of erosion does not stop with the wearing down of mountains into plateaus and hills. As more millions of years pass, the hills too are slowly washed away.

The material that made up the hills and mountains is carried off by streams as silt, sand, and gravel. When the streams leave the steep slopes, they deposit the gravel along their banks. The sand and silt are carried farther, but at last they too are dropped. The result is a flat plain running away from the crumbling hills and mountains.

Many plains are truly impressive. The Great Plains of North America extend over the larger part of ten states and across three Canadian provinces. The Great Northern European Plain sweeps across the west coasts of France and the Low Countries, through northern Germany, Poland, and Russia, to the Ural Mountains, and beyond into Asia. There is a mighty plain in Australia and another across northern India and Pakistan. Perhaps the grandest of all plains is the Russian Steppes—an almost boundless expanse of land that carries the eye unimaginable distances.

The earth's face consists of more than mountains, hills, and plains. Sometimes continental collisions have raised huge flatlands in single massive blocks. These blocks have not tilted to form mountains, but instead have remained flat. They are therefore called plateaus, from the old French word *plat,* "a flat thing."

There are several types of plateaus. Some have been pushed up to tremendous heights. The plateau of Tibet is three miles (4.82 kilometers) in altitude! Here the thin air of the wild

The Rocky Mountains of western North America are rightfully named. Their craggy, snowcapped peaks are the kind usually seen in "new" mountain ranges.

The earth's features range from smooth to rugged. Mountain peaks pierce the sky along many coasts. Beside or between mountains are tablelike landforms called plateaus. Rivers tumble from the fall line, or edge of a plateau, to the lowlands. Broad, flat plains are sometimes broken by the jagged, snowcapped peaks of "new" mountains, or by the low, rounded summits of "old" mountains. Coastal plains have no mountains at all. They stretch—seemingly without end—for miles and miles along the ocean.

ocean   coastal range   intermontane (between mountains) plateau   new mountains

The Alps are Europe's longest mountain range. They stretch some 600 miles (1,014 kilometers) across Italy, France, Switzerland, Austria, and Yugoslavia. Between the peaks, 1,200 glaciers grind their way downhill, moving less than a foot (30 centimeters) a day.

Not even the tallest mountain can stand up under snow, ice, rain, and wind, which pound the solid rock until it breaks into small pieces. Rushing streams carry the stones, gravel, and sand downhill. In time, hills and then a flat plain appear at the foot of the crumbling peak.

Himalaya Mountains forever whistles across the long level expanses. The Altiplano of the Andes is a similarly lofty plateau where big-lunged Peruvians and Bolivians, who can breathe the oxygen-thin air, hack out their farms. About half as high are the plateaus of central Mexico and the Great Basin of the American West. Most Swiss live on the low Swiss Plateau, which is hemmed in by the Jura Mountains and the Alps. Such a plateau is called intermontane (or intermountain) because it lies between mountains.

Sometimes a country consists almost entirely of a plateau. Such is the case with Spain, Turkey, and Iran. Other countries together occupy a single large plateau. The Arabian plateau, for example, includes Israel, Saudi Arabia, Jordan, Lebanon, and Syria. One plateau is so huge that it makes up nearly an entire continent. This is the vast African plateau.

Nothing on the face of the earth is permanent. Plateaus—like all landforms —are constantly being cut up by ice, water, and wind. One day millions of years from now all that will remain of even the largest plateau will be a series of lonely buttes, much like the formations in Arizona's haunting Monument Valley.

Yes, the earth has many faces: hills, mountains, plains, and plateaus. All are part of our changing world.

plain

old mountains

piedmont
(foot of the mountain)
plateau

fall line

coastal plain

ocean

Naming the Land

When the land was formed, no part of it had a name. Then prehistoric tribes began filing through the mountain passes and across the broad plains. They gazed in awe at certain peaks and called them the high places, or the Alps. Other tribes in another land gasped at a mighty range with its rocky castles of ice and called it the snow dwelling, or Himalaya.

Rivers too were wonderous things, moving and sparkling as if they were alive. Tribes in North America watched a band of water curving gracefully through oak-covered hills and called it the Ohio, or beautiful river. And west of the Ohio was the huge river into which all others seemed to flow. The people named it the Mississippi, or big river.

But naming the mountains and rivers was not enough. Ancient peoples had to have some way to identify the whole territory around them. And so the Greeks of long ago called the continent to the east of them Asia, from the Assyrian word *Asu*, "the sunrise." The continent to the west of them they called Europe, from the Assyrian word *Ereb*, "the sunset."

Still, simply giving names to great

Many lands were named for the tribes who once lived there. The British Isles received their name from the ancient Britons who covered themselves with blue warpaint and fought in dagger-spiked chariots. In the mid-400s, the Anglo-Saxons conquered much of Britain. That part was then called Angle-land, or England.

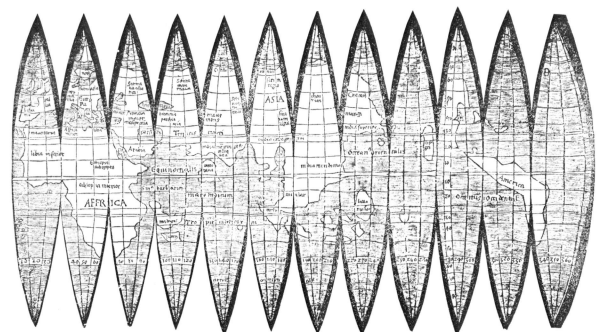

The first map with the name America on it was published in 1507 by Martin Waldseemuller, a German mapmaker. He chose the name to honor Amerigo Vespucci, an Italian explorer who, in 1497, claimed he had discovered a new continent. Columbus had reached the New World five years earlier, but didn't know it. He thought he had found a new route to the Indies.

continental areas did not satisfy the Greeks and other peoples. Territories were further identified by the names of the tribes who lived in them. Thus France received its name. For centuries the area was called Gaul, after the inhabitants. But when the warlike Franks overthrew the Gauls, the area became known as France.

Perhaps one of the oddest place-namings belongs to Russia. The Rus was a family group, not even a major tribe. They called in the Vikings to help them in their wars and it was the Vikings, more than the Rus, who eventually formed the first Russian state.

The Vikings also had their hand in North America. Several hundred years before Columbus they are believed to have founded a colony either in Newfoundland, Canada, or near Cape Cod. They called the area Vinland, for grapevines grew there.

The Viking name did not stick. But neither was America named for Columbus, who rediscovered it. Instead a German mapmaker decided to call it after Amerigo Vespucci, an Italian explorer. Amerigo sailed to the continent in 1497 and realized he had reached a new world, while Columbus was still telling everyone the land he had found five years earlier was part of Asia.

Antarctica received its name in a backhanded way. The word means nothing more than "opposite of the Arctic." The Arctic, for its part, was named by our friends the ancient Greeks, who referred to it as the place under *arktikos,* the bear constellations. Two stars in the Great Bear do, in fact, point to the North Star, which wags the tip of the Little Bear's cold tail.

Many places were named after kings and queens. The Philippine Islands honor King Philip of Spain. The state of Georgia honors King George of Britain—and Virginia is named for Elizabeth I, the Virgin Queen of Britain. Alexandria, Egypt, honors Alexander, the young military genius from Macedonia.

Every piece of land has a name, and some have had many, since each passing tribe gave the land a new name. Every name, old or new, tells a tale.

Australia, the great island continent, was only legend until Dutch sailors sighted the sandy shore in 1606. Before that, the continent was called Terra Australis Incognita, or Unknown Southern Land.

Many places are named by chance and keep those names by custom. A Spanish explorer came upon a great body of water and called it the Gulf of Mexico. Halfway around the world a sea captain sailed what he called the East China Sea. The bodies of water are alike in size, but people still call one a gulf and the other a sea.

Getting Around on a Round Earth

This mariner's astrolabe, probably belonging to a Spanish sailor, dates back to 1585. It was found in 1845 under a rock on the Irish coast, near the spot where three Spanish ships sank in 1588.

Early maps were simply crude charcoal sketches on pieces of cloth which the Latins, an ancient people, called mappas. In the Middle Ages, the drawings themselves became known as mappas or maps.

More than 2,000 years ago the islanders of Micronesia, in the South Pacific, navigated the open seas between the islands. They used stick charts, called mattangs. The sticks were so placed as to show ocean swells and wave patterns.

We do not know how maps first came into being, but it was probably something like this.

Ancient peoples gazing out across the Mediterranean Sea knew that other tribes lived beyond the water. They wished to visit these peoples in order to trade. To reach these faraway lands they questioned the strangers who sometimes came to their villages. As the strangers described the routes they had taken, village elders sketched the directions with charcoal on pieces of cloth. The Latins, an ancient people, called these cloths *mappa*—and so the drawings became known as *mappas,* or maps.

The first maps gave travelers only the most confusing idea of the world around them. But gradually captains guided their ships farther along the unknown coast of the mysterious sea. As they did, they recorded the capes and headlands passed by, marking them on their cloths, or mappas.

During their voyages the captains found they could steer at night by keeping track of a certain star which did not wheel around the heavens like the sun and other stars. This star always burned almost due north and was accordingly called the North Star, or Polaris.

Not only did Polaris always glitter in the north, but it rose slowly over a period of nights as one sailed toward it and fell as one sailed away. Astronomers had long calculated the height of a star by its number of degrees above the horizon. And so the captains began measuring the altitude of the North Star in degrees using a primitive device called an astrolabe. Then, as their ships passed odd-looking hills and other landmarks, the captains wrote the height of Polaris on their maps. This way they could tell a little better where they were and how far they had yet to go.

Eventually ships began to sail

farther into the Mediterranean. Soon captains learned another important fact: the North Star stood at the same height in many locations. Thus, it was thirty-five degrees off the coast of Syria and was also thirty-five degrees off Cyprus. Farther north at Ostia, the port of Rome, the star hovered at forty-two degrees, the same reading that could be recorded off the island of Corsica.

On their maps captains connected all the locations of the same degrees with straight lines. These lines ran parallel to each other. We call them parallels. The distance between them is called latitude.

Placing parallels on ships' maps was a breakthrough in navigation, for captains no longer had to inch along the winding coast. Instead they could plunge into the open water until the North Star stood at, say, thirty-eight degrees if their goal was famed Athens. They then turned east, keeping the North Star always at thirty-eight degrees over their left shoulder until the coast of Greece came into view. "Sailing the parallel" became a favorite navigational technique.

Although vessels had plied the Mediterranean for more than two thousand years before the birth of Christ, it was not until around A.D. 150 that Claudius Ptolemy drew the first maps that have come down to us. Ptolemy, growing up in the bustling seaport of Alexandria, Egypt, probably learned his geography from talkative ship captains, as well as from reading scrolls deposited in Alexandria's huge library.

In many ways Ptolemy's maps were surprisingly modern—they portrayed the earth as round. The parallels were close to those measured by modern instruments, and the lands around the Mediterranean were drawn in shapes we would recognize today.

But Ptolemy shared the problem of all ancient mapmakers. With the aid of Polaris, he could measure a city's location north or south. But he had no way of telling how far east or west it was.

Really good maps had to wait for the development of the idea of longitude. That didn't happen until more than a thousand years later.

Early mariners "sailed the parallel." A captain might leave Genoa, Italy, and sail in a southerly direction until the North Star shown 35 degrees above the horizon. He then sailed an imaginary line due east, always keeping the star at 35 degrees over his left shoulder, until the isle of Crete loomed ahead.

In the late 1400s mariners ventured out on the open seas with the help of an astrolabe. Through its sights they measured in degrees the height of the North Star above the horizon. The higher the star, the greater the number of degrees, and the farther north the ship had sailed.

Mapping the Whole World

Parallels

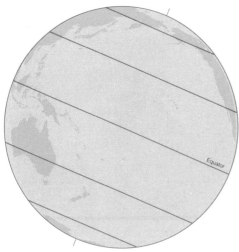

Parallels run in an east-west direction around the globe. They measure distance north and south of the equator, called latitude, in degrees.

Meridians

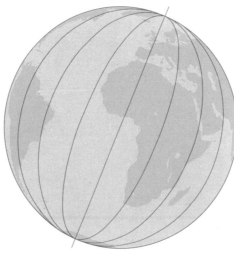

Meridians run north and south between the two poles. The distance east or west between meridians is called longitude. Longitude is measured in degrees, too.

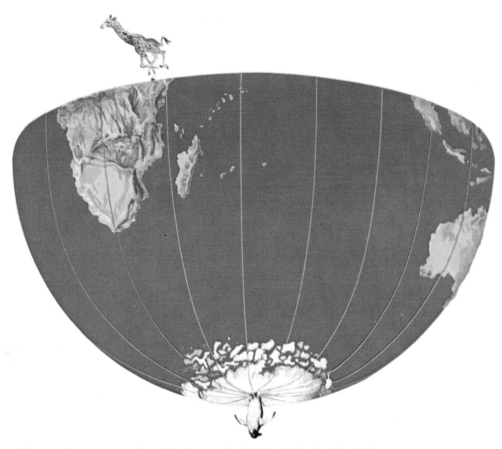

Distance between meridians shrinks near the North and South poles. At the equator, a giraffe would have to run seventy miles (112.65 kilometers) to cover one degree of longitude. Near the South Pole, a penguin could merely wiggle a toe over the ice and cross a meridian.

It must have been an eerie feeling to be on a ship at night on the open sea before the days of good maps. Dark water slapped at the hull. A wind pounded the sails as the ship churned forward. A sailor could get no hint of what lay ahead in the blackness.

How far had the ship traveled while "sailing the parallel"? Had it gone faster and farther than the crew had guessed? Did a rocky shore loom just ahead?

What was needed to tell distances traveled east or west were maps with lines running north and south much the way parallels ran crossways. Such lines would cross the parallels at regular intervals, giving a way of measuring distance traveled on any one parallel.

The need for such maps became particularly important after Columbus's voyage to the New World in 1492. It was vital for travelers crossing the Atlantic to know how far east or west they had sailed so that they would know how to ration their food.

In theory there was nothing difficult about the idea of meridians to measure east-west distance. The earth's rotation caused the sun to make a circle of 360 degrees around the heavens every twenty-four hours. By dividing 360 degrees by twenty-four, astronomers figured out that the sun seemed to move 15 degrees every hour. Mapmakers picked up the information.

Thus, when the sun was at its noon-time high in England, fifteen degrees farther west it would be one hour before noon. With this knowledge a ship's captain need only set his clock to English time and sail west. When the sun above him reached its twelve o'clock high, its meridian, but his clock told him it was one o'clock in England, he knew he was fifteen degrees from London.

The problem was that no clock anywhere could withstand the pitch of a ship on the stormy Atlantic.

Philip II, monarch of mighty Spain, offered 1,000 crowns for a seaworthy clock. But a hundred years passed and nobody could make one. Then Britain offered 20,000 pounds ($80,000) and in 1760 one John Harrison claimed the prize. His clock was called a

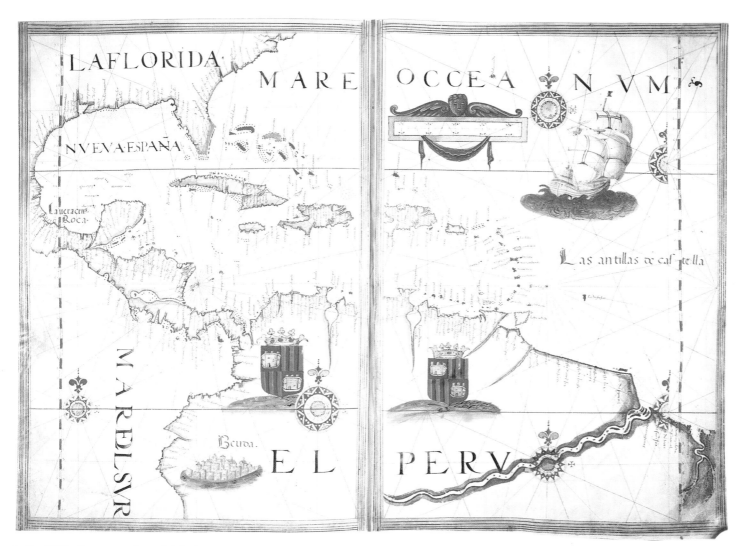

In the 1500s Europeans drew detailed maps, called portolan charts, to guide their ships at sea. Diagonal lines on these charts met at a center point called a compass rose. Each point on the rose showed a direction; navigators charted a course and followed the lines to their ports.

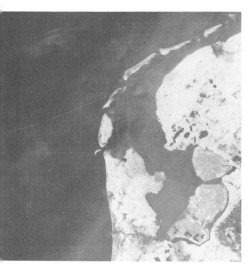

This photo of the Netherlands was taken from space using special film. Warm areas—vegetation—show up as red. Cooler areas —cities and sea—are blue. The light blue patch, lower right, will soon become solid ground as the sea is drained from the land.

chronometer. From then on all ships with chronometers could measure their east-west distance from home port.

But where did the meridians start? There was no natural zero, for every inch of the earth had a noontime meridian. Each seagoing nation urged that its capital be named zero. But in 1884 an international conference gave the honor to Britain as the most important maritime nation; the Royal Observatory at Greenwich just outside London became the "Prime" Meridian, zero.

With Greenwich as zero, the meridians marched step by step around the world. The tenth meridian west was in Ireland and the tenth meridian east was in Germany. The meridians continued both east and west until they met at 180 degrees in the Pacific.

The establishment of a grid of parallels and meridians did not stop here. Soon each degree east or west, north or south, was broken down into sixty parts called minutes. These minutes were divided still further into seconds. A second of latitude was so precise that it could position any place on the globe to within 101 feet (30.78 meters). Now, for the first time, it was possible to draw really accurate maps. By the beginning of the twentieth century almost every government had surveyors taking latitude and longitude readings and constructing maps of their territories.

Not long after the invention of the airplane and the camera, aerial photographs began to be used in mapping. This greatly increased the speed, as well as the accuracy, with which maps could be made. Surveyors no longer had to comb on foot every inch of land to be mapped.

Modern maps have come a long way from the days when village elders scratched directions on wrinkled mappa cloths.

A Map is a Map, Not a Photograph

To astronauts circling high above the earth, the world looks like a gigantic, bluish ball. The oceans are huge expanses of blue, with fringes of pale green where the water is shallow. Islands have necklaces of silvery waves crashing around them. Jungles are somber shades of green. Deserts reflect the tans and reddish browns of bare rocks in brilliant sunshine. Cities are blobs of smoky haze.

While modern maps are like rocket-ship views of the earth, they are far superior to what astronauts actually see. Persons in space float over cities, but they do not know how many people live in them. They see great chunks of land, but cannot tell what nations occupy them. They view large agricultural areas, but they have no idea what crops grow there.

Maps can tell all these facts—and many, many more.

For example, there are several methods cartographers use to show how many people live in a city. One is to indicate little towns by a dot, bigger towns with a circle around a dot, and major cities with their actual shapes colored yellow.

Or cartographers can show a town's size by the size of the type used to spell its name. Small type indicates small towns and large type represents large towns.

Cartographers can also give a lot of information by means of colors. Blue usually represents oceans and lakes—just as it does to astronauts. But, in addition, blues of various shades can indicate ocean depth; something astronauts cannot see.

On some maps colors show heights. Usually green is for low country and plains, tan is for plateaus and low mountains, and brown is for higher mountains. Really high peaks are tipped with white to show snowcaps.

Sometimes colors are used to show temperatures. Blue usually indicates cooler temperatures, and various shades of red indicate warmer temperatures. A map of summer temperatures will thus contain mainly reds and a winter map will show mostly blues.

Many maps rely more on drawings than colors. A series of small lines, called shading, make mountains appear to jut from the paper. Forests are shown by the tops of trees, deserts by sand dunes, polar regions by glaciers and ice caps.

A precise way to give elevation is by means of contour maps. On these maps all the land of a certain height is connected by a line. Then all land, say, 100 feet (30.48 meters) higher is connected by another line. Some-

You enter a zoo. Where are the gorillas? you ask. A map like the one at right would help you. Paths are marked. You would follow the path away from the entrance to the gorillas' habitat.

times the result is a series of lines that roughly circle particular regions. Contour lines close together indicate rapid rises or dips in elevation. Lines far apart indicate an area of very little change, such as a flat prairie.

Maps are of so many varieties, and show so many different facts, that most cartographers explain what they are doing in small tables of symbols called legends.

One of a legend's most important jobs is to show the scale of the map. The scale indicates the amount that the real size of the earth has been reduced to fit onto a piece of paper. On some maps a thousand miles has become no longer than a fingernail!

To indicate the scale used, many legends state something like: "One inch represents ten miles." Others use a bar like this:

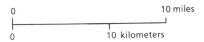

Some maps also have a drawing at one corner that points out directions. Usually this is not necessary, for nearly every map has north at the top. This may go back to the ancient sea captains who looked upward to Polaris as they set their directions.

With north at the top of the map, south will naturally be at the bottom. East will be to the right and west to the left, just as they are on a compass.

Mapmakers have done amazing things. They have taken the huge earth, 24,902.45 miles (40,075.61 kilometers) in circumference, and reduced it to the size of a piece of paper. More than that, they have supplied information on a tremendous variety of subjects. From one detailed map we can learn more about the earth in an hour than astronauts staring out their window could learn in a thousand space orbits.

To see how scale works, measure your room. On paper, draw one inch for each foot you measured. You can map anything—your yard, your block, your school playground.

If you could rise in a helicopter above a zoo, the zoo would soon become a blur. Everything around it would blend together.

A map of the same area would point out the zoo and even the names of the roads leading to it. Confusing details would be left out.

Water Almost Everywhere

The ocean waves begin far offshore. They roll and cascade, their tops sparkling in the sunshine. At last they fling themselves against the sandy beach. They toss up starfish and seashells, then slide away with a sighing undertow.

Beyond the place where the waves break, the water lies darkly mysterious.

Most persons know little of the water beyond the beaches. Yet oceans, seas, and lakes occupy three-fourths of the earth's surface.

The great water empire begins gently just offshore. Here the sea is a garden where unusual plants and animals thrive in the sunlight that filters through the shallow water. In tropical waters these creatures of the sea often have bright colors, such as those of the brilliant redbeard sponge, the flowerlike anemone, and the purple seafan.

Farther out, the water becomes deeper and the sunlight entering it is dimmed. Sharks and other large fish glide dangerously among the long chains of brown kelp that grow 100 feet (30.48 meters) or longer. The waves are large and menacing. Yet the surface of the churning water is alive

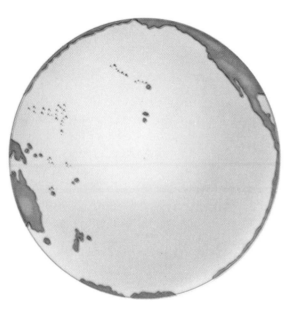

Water covers nearly three-fourths of the globe. When the earth was born it was covered by an even 1½ miles (2.4 kilometers) of water. Our planet has lost little or no moisture since then. Trapped as vapor in the atmosphere, water returns to earth as rain or snow.

In the North Pacific between Alaska and Siberia lies the giant Aleutian Trench. It is over 24,000 feet (7,315 meters) deep and was formed about 100 million years ago when the seabed cracked. Volcanoes erupted on the north side of the trench and piled up lava to build the Aleutian Islands. The volcanoes are still active.

with billions of microscopic plankton which form the basic food in the chain of life.

The sea bottom falls gradually until it reaches a depth of around 450 feet (136.16 meters). This is the edge of the continental shelf. Now there is a sudden drop-off. More than two miles (3.21 kilometers) nearly straight down lies the wide plain that forms much of the ocean floor.

The ocean plains, which extend for hundreds of miles, are dark, for almost no sunlight can penetrate the depths of water. At intervals huge, largely extinct volcanoes rise up in gloomy conical mounds. Often their tops reach above the waves to form green islands.

In every ocean the plains end at the foot of long underwater mountain ridges. These ridges, which are several miles high, run in regular patterns between the continents. The Mid-Atlantic Ridge makes a lazy S as it arches north to south from the Arctic Circle to Antarctica.

On the other side of the world the East Pacific Rise parallels the entire coast of South America.

The ocean ridges formed as the continental plates moved away from each other. The earth's crust between the plates slowly ripped apart and lava oozed through the opening. Sometimes lava reached above the ocean surface, where it cooled to become a strange island. Thus Iceland, on the chilly arctic border, was born. Even today hot volcanoes spit steam and molten rock into the sub-zero air.

There are also immense trenches in the ocean bottom that cut steeply into the earth's crust. They were formed when one plate rode over the edge of another, forcing it down.

Parts of the continents seen only by divers are the continental shelves. They drop gently away from shore to a depth of about 450 feet (137 meters). Fossils of mastodon, mammoth, and other prehistoric land animals have been found in the ancient streambeds, cliffs, and beaches of the watery continental shelves.

Some trenches extend an astounding six miles (9.65 kilometers) or more downward from sea level. At this great depth the water pressure is so intense that a human body without protection would be squashed like jelly.

The only major trench in the Atlantic is off the island of Puerto Rico. The really awesome trenches are in the Pacific area. There is a steep trench off southwestern Alaska and another off Japan. But the grandest of all is the famed Mariana Trench, the earth's most terrifying canyon. The trench is so deep that Mount Everest, the tallest mountain, could be dropped into it and completely disappear—its peak covered by nearly a mile of water.

Parts of the ocean bottom are more rugged than the continental landscape. It is a truly stupendous world that only maps can show us.

Colonies of coral sometimes grow around volcanic islands. When an island dies and sinks, the coral reef grows into a barrier reef that surrounds a shallow lagoon. The volcanic island finally disappears, and a ring of flat coral is left. It is called an atoll.

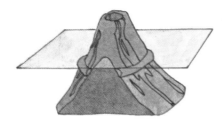
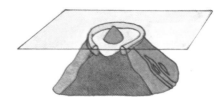
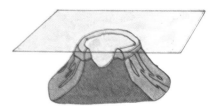

The Sky World

On summer afternoons the wind blows so softly it hardly ruffles the most delicate flower. Clouds float overhead like clusters of silver balloons. It is so peaceful that people are not aware they live at the bottom of a vast, active ocean of air.

But when storms strike, the power of the sky is there for all to see. Lightning spears are hurled earthward. Thunder booms like bombshells. The sun is blotted out by black clouds higher than the Alps. Rain splatters violently against the ground. And mighty winds snap tree limbs and tear doors off their hinges.

The atmosphere that flows around us is invisible. Yet it is surprisingly heavy. If all the air in a small room could be gathered into a ball, the ball would thud against the floor with a weight of about seventy-five pounds (34.02 kilograms).

Traces of the atmosphere extend 5,000 miles (8,046.5 kilometers) into space, but most of the air is concentrated within twelve miles (19.31 kilometers) of the earth's surface.

Looking into a blue sky, it is easy to imagine the atmosphere as a simple mass of clear, calm gases. But this is not the case. The sky has towering mountains of air—and plunging valleys—and streams of wind that flow like rivers. The sky has great waves like those of the ocean—waves that have crests and depressions. The sky has cloud-islands that drift on layers of air. Wide updrafts of warm winds grow and spread like six-mile-high plants. And downdrafts drop earthward to flatten out against the land as if they were spoonfuls of pancake batter.

The reason for all this activity in the sky is the fact that warm air and cold air tend to form into what are called "air masses." Warm air masses usually form in places that are hot for long periods of time. One of the best-known areas for this formation is over the Atlantic Ocean between Africa and the southern United States. Warm air

Every cloud has a special name. Fluffy white ones are cumulus. High, curly wisps of white form cirrus clouds. Stratus cover the sky with an even gray sheet. And dark gray nimbus clouds shower the earth with rain.

masses also form above desert areas—such as Africa's Sahara and Australia's Great Sandy, Gibson, and Victoria deserts.

Cold air masses gather above the frosty tundra in northern Canada and Russian Siberia. They also form in the arctic zones.

From time to time large chunks of air break away from the area where they form. These freed air masses are like huge invisible mountains several thousand feet high and several hundred miles wide. As they move about, they pass right through buildings and over people. No one can see these wandering air masses, but instruments called barometers can measure them. A simple kind of barometer is a column of mercury in a vacuum tube. Normally the mercury stands about thirty inches (76.2 centimeters) high. But when a mountain

A Kind of Barometer

The glass tube is open at one end and filled with mercury. The open end rests in a dish, allowing some of the mercury to escape. Air pushes down on the mercury in the dish. When air pressure is great, the mercury is forced up into the tube to about 31 inches (78.74 centimeters). The weather is fair. When air pressure is less, mercury in the dish rises, but it falls within the tube. Stormy weather may follow.

of air is overhead, the mercury is pushed up to about thirty-one inches (78.74 centimeters).

The warm and the cold air masses usually collide in a battle area called a frontal zone. In the Northern Hemisphere, this zone is generally between thirty and sixty degrees latitude and includes most of Europe, the United States, Canada, and Japan.

When the two systems meet, the cool air swirls against the warm, pushing the warm air upward. The warm air cools and can no longer hold as much water vapor as before. The vapor condenses into clouds. As the clouds grow more dense, the moisture falls as rain or snow. Thus the meeting of cold and warm air masses usually results in stormy weather.

The air masses continue to swirl about each other, gradually mixing until they hardly exist as separate masses. The storm then breaks up.

Meanwhile, new warm and cold air masses break away from the areas where they have formed and move toward the frontal zone.

The drama of the sky continues.

Tornadoes strike swiftly and with little warning. Winds at the spinning center may reach 300 miles (480 kilometers) per hour. Huge updrafts of air in the funnel can uproot large trees and toss cars and other heavy things hundreds of feet.

A hurricane can slam into shore with winds of up to 150 miles (241 kilometers) per hour. Winds, sea, and driving rain produce huge waves that flood the land. Suddenly the "eye" or center of the storm passes overhead bringing a deadly calm. Less than an hour later, the other side of the storm strikes with new fury.

23

One World

The land, the oceans, and the atmosphere are parts of a single unit: the earth. Events in one area nearly always affect events in the other two. This is how the interaction works. Sunlight flashing through the atmosphere warms the land and the oceans. Air currents then absorb the heat and flow outward. On the way, they pick up water vapor from the seas and lakes and tiny bits of dust from the land. The vapor, forced upward, cools and condenses around the dust to form raindrops. The rain falls to earth where it waters the plants and refills the oceans.

Sunlight, water, dust, and wind—all are required for the cycle of rain. Should any part of this chain break, rain would cease to fall and life on the land would vanish.

There are other vital interchanges between the land, the oceans, and the air. One of the most important is the distribution of heat.

Were it not for movements of the air and oceans, the whole area around the equator would be unbelievably hot. On the other hand, northern lands, such as Great Britain, Norway, Sweden, and Canada, would be bleak snowfields most of the time. Weather systems and ocean currents, like the famous Gulf Stream, constantly mix

From space the earth looks like a great, colorful ball. Air, land, and water seem mixed without rhyme or reason. But these parts together create the delicate balance that makes life possible.

The Gulf Stream, flowing northeast across the Atlantic, feeds its warm waters into the North Atlantic Current which greatly affects the climate of northwestern Europe. Many ports remain ice free all winter. London is much farther north than New York, but it has an average January temperature nearly ten degrees warmer.

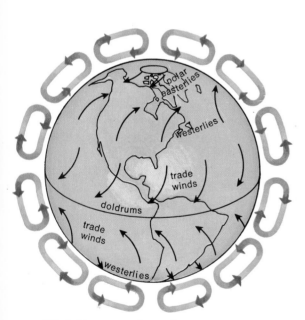

Winds blow across the earth in set patterns. Trade winds move southwest and northwest toward the equator. Westerlies waft out of the west and polar easterlies gust from the east. But dead calm rules where the air rises at the doldrums and falls at the horse latitudes.

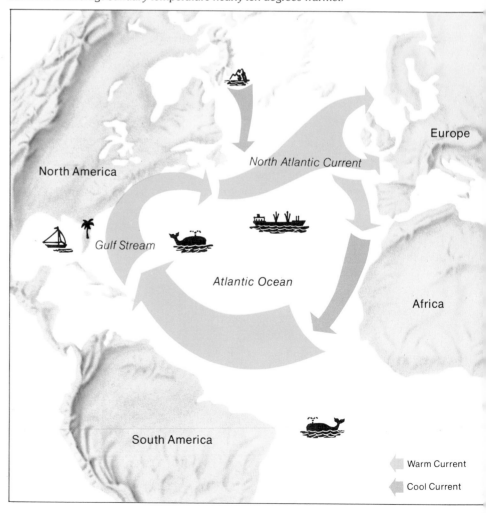

hot and cold so that most areas are neither too warm nor too cool.

The atmosphere also has a very close relationship with the land and the seas. When the earth was young, the air was composed of deadly methane and ammonia gases. Gradually, however, blue-green algae appeared that could produce oxygen. After a billion years, the algae made enough oxygen for the first primitive oxygen-breathing animals to come into existence.

Oxygen is an almost magical element. Not only do land animals depend on it for life, but it is absorbed into water where fish and other sea animals breathe it. It also circulates high into the atmosphere, where it changes into the layer of ozone gas which filters out cosmic rays that are harmful to land life.

Thus, while we often think of the land, oceans, and atmosphere as being separate, they are not. The early mapmakers knew this. They drew their parallels and meridians circling the globe, over land as well as through the water. And these parallels and meridians had their origin in the sky—for they were based on observations of the heavens.

Land, water, and air work together to support life. Animals breathe in oxygen and give off carbon dioxide. Plants take in carbon dioxide and water and give off oxygen and water vapor. Vapor rises from the sea, mixes with dust to form clouds, and rain occurs. The seas are renewed, plants are watered, and the cycle begins anew.

Pollution of air, water, and land endangers all forms of life. Smog—a mixture of smoke, fog, and poisonous gases—strikes many cities. Below, a dirty, yellow orange smog hangs over Havana, Cuba.

The Earth Abounds

Rice is a basic food to Asian peoples. They strain their backs for long hours tending the plants. These paddies in the Philippines cover nearly every inch of the hilly land.

Hold a seed in your hand. It seems cold and lifeless. But place it in the earth and watch the wonder of growth. From the rough shell comes tender white roots, a graceful stem, and green leaves that reach eagerly into the sunshine.

Of all the good things that come from the earth, three crops in particular have been of the greatest importance to humanity. They are the grains wheat, rice, and corn.

Wheat has had a tremendous effect on the human race for more than eight thousand years. Learning to grow it rather than gathering it wild was a big step for early people. Made into bread it became, and still is, the basic food for half the world.

Bread's advantage was that it did not spoil like fruit or meat. Therefore ancient peoples could build up extra supplies of food. And since they didn't have to spend all their time farming, some people could engage in other activities. They could make new products, write books, erect cities with towers that reached for the sky. In short, they could create civilizations.

What wheat is to most of the world,

Most corn is fed to farm animals, but people enjoy sweet corn, popcorn, and foods made from cornmeal, like Latin American tortillas. Rice is the chief food of about half the world. Many Asians eat rice three times a day, often with little else. Most other peoples eat wheat bread and other wheat products. In fact, all the wheat grown in just one year would fill a huge freight train reaching more than twice around the earth.

rice is to Asia. Both grains are members of the grass family, but rice can grow in rainy, hot climates where wheat cannot. Like wheat, rice helped make civilizations possible since it could be stored for future use.

Rice is planted in paddies, which are shallow ponds dug by hand. When the grain is ripe, the paddies are drained and the rice is removed from the stalk by threshing. It is then boiled and eaten—usually with wooden chopsticks. China produces almost half of the world's rice. It is also an important food in all of the nations in South Asia and in Japan.

Of these three major crops, perhaps corn has the most interesting history. The American Indians worshiped the Corn Spirit, who was a golden-haired youth. It is believed corn, also called maize, was strictly a product of the New World. Europeans did not know about the grain until Christopher Columbus returned from his voyages and showed it to them.

Corn is still grown mainly in the New World. The great Corn Belt reaches across the United States from Ohio to the edge of the Great Plains—almost a thousand miles (1,609.3 kilometers) of green and gold. Although sweet corn can be a delicious part of a late summer meal, most corn is of a kind which is given to farm animals. Corn-fed beef and pork are important sources of protein throughout much of the world.

Human beings depend not only on food for survival, but also on clothing for protection against the climate. Most clothing is composed all or in part of cotton.

Cotton plants have seeds that develop within an odd circular cage called a boll. In late summer the boll breaks open, exposing the fuzzy white fibers that surround the seeds. The fibers are spun together by machines to make thread. The thread, in turn, is woven into cloth that is stitched into shirts, blouses, coats, and other clothing.

The earth also furnishes the minerals that are necessary for modern civilization. Most important of these minerals is iron.

Iron was probably discovered by ancient people who found it as a strange molten material glowing beneath the logs of a once-roaring fire. The heat had

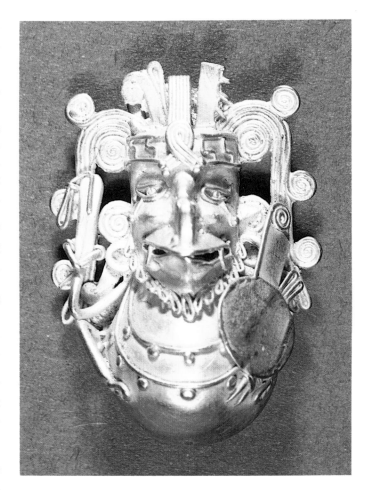

melted the iron ore rocks upon which the fire had been built. The ancients could hammer the hot iron into many useful items, such as tools, horseshoes, and nails. The beginning of the Iron Age was a major milestone in the progress of humanity. And we are involved in the Iron Age to this day.

Steel is a mixture of iron and small amounts of carbon and other materials. It is probably the most useful metal of modern times. Nearly everything from cars to the girders which support skyscrapers are made mostly of steel.

The industrial might of a nation is partly measured by its production of steel. The Soviet Union forges the most steel—twenty-four percent of the world total. Japan produces about sixteen percent. It is followed by the United States with ten percent, China with eight percent, and West Germany with six percent. Together the five nations account for two-thirds of the whole world's production!

The good earth is our natural storehouse. We must be careful never to destroy the fertility and productivity of the land upon which we live.

The gold figure at left was made in Mexico before the time of Columbus. Through the ages people have craved gold because its bright color never tarnishes. Heated, it is soft and easy to shape into truly dazzling decorations.

Iron ore and other materials from the earth formed the steel beams of the world's first skyscraper—Chicago's Home Insurance Building, built in 1885. Today, Chicago's steel and glass Sears' Tower soars 110 stories—the tallest building in the world.

Energy/Our Resources

Listen to the throb of a finely tuned racing car engine. Within each cylinder the piston flies up and down with blinding speed. When the driver slams the car into gear, the machine whines to a start. Within seconds it is hurtling down the track like a cannon shot.

This is power! And behind the power is the energy that exists in the fuel that drives the engine.

Energy is defined as anything that is able to do work. Human muscles can perform tasks only by using the energy furnished by food.

For hundreds of thousands of years the only energy source humans used was food. Work meant sweat and aching muscles.

The breakthrough in energy came around 1700 when inventors discovered that coal released a tremendous amount of energy when it was set on fire. The blue-hot flames could cause water to boil, and the steam from this boiling water could drive engines. The Industrial Revolution was born.

In the mid-1800s an even more important source of energy began to be recognized. This was the black, sticky oil which leaked out of the earth in many places. Using a process called cracking, crude oil, also known as petroleum, could be made into gasoline. This set the stage for the development of many industries including those for the airplane and automobile.

Crude oil also can be made into fuel oil. Fuel oil not only heats furnaces but also runs machinery which makes everything from the clothes we wear to the television sets we watch.

Another source of energy almost as important as coal and oil is natural gas. It is usually found in the same drilling areas which produce crude oil. Natural gas is used to heat homes. It is often pumped through underground pipes from gas fields as far as two thousand miles (3,218.6 kilometers) away.

The energy from oil, natural gas, and coal also turns the massive generators which provide us with electricity. Take away these high-energy fuels and the generators would grind to a halt.

Industrial nations depend heavily upon oil, natural gas, and coal for their energy needs. Many attempts have been made to find other sources of energy. Energy from the sun and from the wind have been experimented with, but these have not yet proven their worth on a large scale. Nuclear reactors, too, can generate electricity—and there are over 150 of them around the world. But the safety of nuclear power plants and the problem of how to dispose of radioactive nuclear wastes leaves the future of such energy in doubt. Hydroelectric power, or energy produced from waterpower, is another source of

The Alaskan pipeline runs 800 miles (1,287.44 kilometers) from the frigid Prudhoe Bay oil fields of northern Alaska to the port of Valdez. So that 600,000 caribou can continue their migration, the pipe has been forced into the frozen earth in twenty-four places. The animals walk over the buried pipeline while the valuable oil flows on its way. In just 30 years the Prudhoe oil will be used up.

energy. Water tumbling down through openings in high dams can turn generators at the base of the dam, producing electricity. But hydroelectric plants are very expensive to build, so this source of energy has only been used where water is plentiful and where large amounts of electricity are needed—near cities and industrial areas. Several European countries and Japan have developed hydroelectric power almost to the limits of their water resources.

What are the chances that the world will run out of energy? Many experts predict that our supply of oil will run short in just twenty-five years. And they also say that our natural gas will probably be pretty much used up in just fifty years!

Our supply of coal will last for hundreds of years. But many people warn that burning coal will have a bad effect on our atmosphere.

So what will happen? Will there come a day when all the lights will go out? Will cars be abandoned and will people go back to riding horses and bicycles for transportation?

It seems unlikely, for human beings are an inventive breed who can surely come up with other sources of energy. Perhaps solar heat will do the job. Or perhaps we can perfect microwave energy transmitters based in outer space.

But whatever scientists come up with, our supplies of oil and natural gas shrink each time someone starts a car or lights a furnace. Energy is a precious resource that we must conserve. For if we waste it, it may never be ours again.

Coal drives the antique English steam locomotive. Wind spins the turbine to make electricity. Food powers the muscles that turn the bicycle wheels. These fuels will be used more and more as oil grows scarce.

Energy from the sun, or solar energy, helps heat this house. Water is warmed by the sun's rays, then runs through pipes on the roof and heats the building inside.

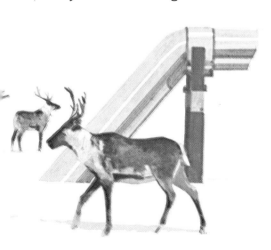

The Oceans/
Our Resources

Big ships churn through the ocean waters. Sometimes angry waves sweep over their decks. Sometimes hurricanes rock them like coconuts in a whirlpool. At other times the ocean is calm and ships cut through it as if they were gliding through a shining liquid mirror. But whatever the condition of the oceans, merchant ships from nearly every country are constantly moving toward faraway ports.

The number of ships sailing the oceans is truly impressive. Nearly twenty-five thousand tankers, bulk carriers and freighters make up the world's fleet. More than half the seaborne trade consists of crude oil.

Ocean shipping is also vital in the transportation of wheat, corn, meat, fruit, and many other products that appear on our dinner tables.

Aside from playing a necessary role in transportation, the ocean is itself an important source of food. Fishing has been a major industry from before the days of the ancient Greeks. Nearly 75 million short tons (68 million metric tons) of fish are taken from the sea each year. Large fleets of fishing vessels voyage as far as ten thousand miles (16,093 kilometers) in search of tuna, whales, and other marine life. Schools of fish can be located by sonar devices. After they are caught, the fish are very often canned or frozen right on board.

The supply of sea animals may seem everlasting, but such is not the case. Overfishing in some areas has resulted in nations declaring restricted zones off their shores. But even with these restrictions, some sea animals, especially certain varieties of whales, are in extreme danger of extinction.

To insure continued supplies, efforts

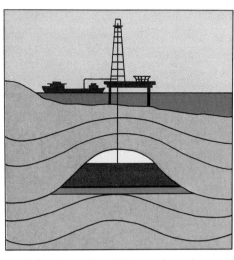

A tall derrick sends a drill down through many feet of water and the ocean floor to reach oil trapped offshore between rocky layers of the continental shelf.

are being made to develop fish "farms." In some of these test stations, fish are raised to finger size in floating cages. They are then released into areas where they grow into adults. The Japanese, in particular, have been successful raising tuna in this way.

An interesting experiment with oysters was carried out in Chesapeake Bay, on the east coast of the United States. It showed that more young oysters reach maturity under controlled conditions than in natural oyster beds. There is hope that such underwater farms may be able to grow many kinds of fish to add to the world's food supply.

The ocean may also be able to furnish us with many minerals. Salt, which makes up about three-fourths of the mineral content of water, has been obtained from the sea for centuries. Another mineral, aragonite, also comes from the ocean floor. This mineral is present in pearls and gives them their beautiful rainbow shine. Aragonite can be used to make cement, glass, and fertilizer. Near Thailand and Indonesia dredgers scoop up cassiterite, from which tin can be refined. Manganese, cobalt, and copper can also be obtained from the ocean.

Oil is a major natural resource found beneath the sea. Most oil exploration has been in the relatively shallow waters near the edges of the continents. One of the most famous underwater oil discoveries was in the North Sea between Britain and Norway. Now offshore drillers are expanding into deeper and deeper waters. Drill ships can successfully reach down to tap oil that lies beyond the shelf drop-off, in the deep seabed, and even on the mid-ocean ridges.

The knowledge of ocean resources is still in the beginning stages. In the future, food, minerals, and energy from the ocean may prove to be major benefits to the human race. Dreamers also talk about future cities under the sea where fish farms and harvests of algae and seaweed would provide food. Transportation would be by submarine sled rather than motorcar. Such a dream seems fantastic today. But tomorrow...who can tell?

Under the Sea Today

A Sonar-equipped fishing ship locates fish by bouncing sound waves off them.
B This drill-ship can bore beneath the ocean floor in search of oil.
C Drill platform houses up to 100 workers. .
D Divers harvest coral and hoist it to the surface in nets.

Underwater City of the Future

E Diver with a tankless suit "breathes" without using his lungs. A tiny cartridge attached to his body transfers oxygen directly into his bloodstream.
F Submarine sled used for exploring—or for racing and other sporting events.
G Fish "huts" contain fish tended by divers or fish "farmers."
H Seawater drawn into this glass dome looses its salt as it is turned to vapor by the sun's heat. The vapor cools to become drinking water.
I A tough, plastic-glass dome protects offices, grocery stores, movie houses, and restaurants.
J Workhorse submarine speeds passengers or cargo along at 230 miles (370.13 kilometers) per hour.
K Oil storage tanks.
L Oil from undersea drillings is pumped to this refinery where it is cleaned for use.

Empty and Crowded Areas

If you were to visit a big city you could feel the almost overwhelming pressure of the crowds. They would squeeze you into elevators and push you into buses. In the air there would be the loud sounds of humanity: cars honking, police whistles blaring, people talking and shouting.

Cities are closely packed. (Geographers say they are "dense.") One of the most crowded is New York City. Here over twenty thousand persons are jammed together in every square mile.

Yet in relation to the amount of land available, the earth is not overly populated. If people could be spread evenly around the globe, there would only be about seventy persons per square mile. Canada has an average of only six persons living in a square mile of land. Alaska averages less than one person per square mile.

Why are some places so empty and others so crowded? It is obvious that few humans can live amid the icy mountains of Antarctica—nor in bleak, windswept places like Siberia or northern Canada. Neither are many people able to survive in the blistering heat of the Sahara or Australian deserts, or in the steamy jungles of central Africa or Brazil.

If you were to examine a special kind of map showing population density, you would be surprised at how much of the earth is unsuitable for large numbers of people. In all the world there are only four major areas of human settlement. These are the China-Japan-Korea triangle, the subcontinent of India, northeastern North America, and most of Europe.

The Asian triangle contains a very high population density. Indeed, Japan has one of the most closely packed populations of any major country anywhere. And China boasts one-fifth of the inhabitants of the entire world!

There are many large cities in this area—among them Shanghai and Peking in China, and Seoul in South Korea. Tokyo, Japan, is the most populated city in the world. It throbs to the life of almost 9 million bustling citizens.

The subcontinent of India, which also includes Pakistan and Bangladesh, is even more densely populated than China. Manufacturing and trade are not well enough developed to support the masses of people, so most of the people live in villages and depend on farming. Even so they cannot grow enough food and the threat of starvation hangs over millions.

Europe is among the world's most important manufacturing and commercial centers. European nations, including the Soviet Union, make more than half the world's goods. The area contains five giant metropolitan, or city, areas of which London, Moscow, and Paris are the largest. Rivers and connecting canals and an immense railroad and highway network link the various countries. Port facilities like those in Rotterdam, in the Netherlands, are among the largest in the world.

The Industrial Revolution began in Europe and from there was carried everywhere by traders. At one time British and French empires spanned the earth. Even today most experts agree that Europe is the hub of the world.

The northeast part of North America is another crowded region. The most populated area stretches from New York and Philadelphia on the east coast inland about 800 miles (1,287.44 kilometers) to Chicago on Lake Michigan. This is the core of the continent. Two-thirds of the industrial workers and forty percent of the population of the United States and Canada live in this area.

Outside of the four principal crowded regions of the earth, there are many other scattered areas of dense population. Among these are Mexico City, fourth largest urban complex in the world; Cairo, in Egypt; São Paulo, Brazil; and Sydney, Australia.

Populations within most countries are fluid. They flow to where the job opportunities are, especially in the more industrialized nations. Only the future will tell us where the crowded areas of tomorrow will develop.

Many people leave their farms and villages and go to the cities looking for jobs and a better life. They may find work, but they are crowded closely together in the noisy towns.

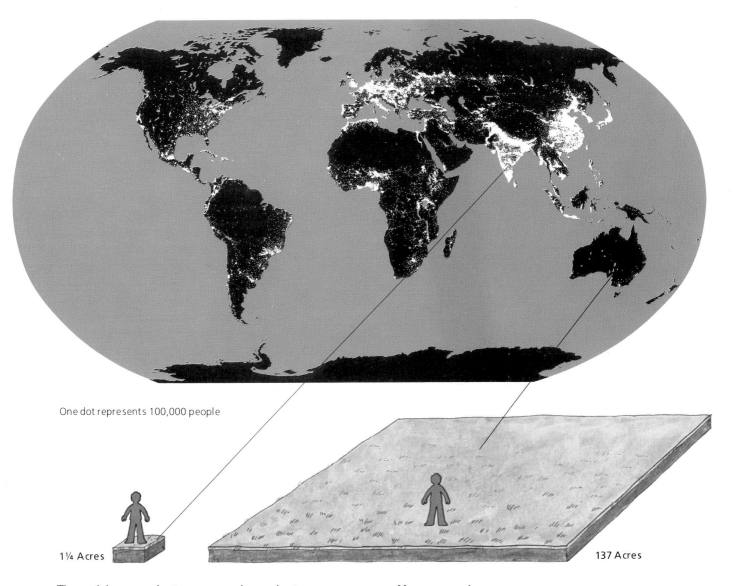

One dot represents 100,000 people

1¼ Acres

137 Acres

The earth has space for its many people, nearly nine acres per person. However, much of the earth is not fit for human life. Through the centuries people have gathered where food can be easily grown. India is such an area. It now has so many people that if the land were divided equally among them each person would have just 1¼ acres. Compare that with Australia. If it were divided, each person would have 137 acres—a hundred times more space, but much of it desert.

Many places on earth are hostile to human life. Few people can survive the cold, barren landscape of Iceland, left. Trees and plants may thrive in the humid Amazon rain forest of Brazil, but few people can live in this disease-ridden tangle of growth.

The World Divided

Human beings do not wander freely about the earth. Barriers are set up by groups of people who speak the same language and have a common history. These are called national—or political —borders.

Almost always, borders are made only after a great deal of bickering between neighbors. Nowhere is this more true than in Europe where so many different nations occupy such a small amount of space. The Great Northern European Plain is occupied by the French, the Belgians, the Dutch, the Germans, the Poles, and the Russians. Over the past centuries almost countless battles, some as large as World Wars I and II, have been fought to determine the exact national borders in this area. Much the same holds true for southeastern Europe. Here the borders of the Soviet Union, Romania, Hungary, Bulgaria, Yugoslavia, and Czechoslovakia have changed many times with the fortunes of war.

National borders have also changed a great deal in that part of Asia known as the Middle East. During the distant past the Babylonians, Egyptians, Persians, and others have had vast empires which have wiped out all other borders. In the early part of the twentieth century the British and French counted much of the

Germany and the Allies fought many terrible battles during World War I. Each side dug hundreds of miles of trenches from which they launched attacks across the battle line.

In 1950, Britian, France, and other European nations controlled much of Africa. But by 1985, fifty-five independent nations had appeared where before there were only four.

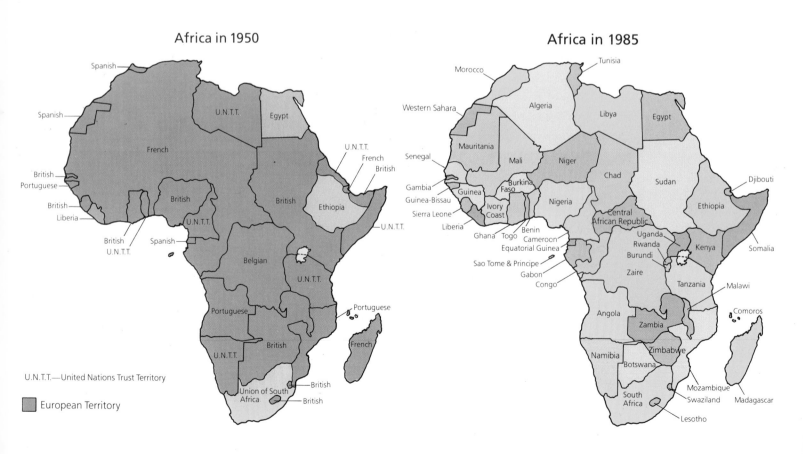

Africa in 1950

Spanish
Spanish
U.N.T.T.
Egypt
French
U.N.T.T.
French
British
British
Portuguese
British
British
Ethiopia
British
Liberia
U.N.T.T.
U.N.T.T.
British
Spanish
Belgian
U.N.T.T.
Portuguese
Portuguese
British
French
U.N.T.T.
British
Union of South Africa
British

U.N.T.T.—United Nations Trust Territory

European Territory

Africa in 1985

Morocco
Tunisia
Western Sahara
Algeria
Libya
Egypt
Mauritania
Senegal
Mali
Niger
Chad
Sudan
Djibouti
Gambia
Burkina Faso
Guinea
Guinea-Bissau
Nigeria
Ethiopia
Ivory Coast
Central African Republic
Sierra Leone
Liberia
Ghana
Togo
Benin
Cameroon
Uganda
Equatorial Guinea
Rwanda
Kenya
Somalia
Sao Tome & Principe
Burundi
Gabon
Zaire
Congo
Tanzania
Malawi
Comoros
Angola
Zambia
Zimbabwe
Namibia
Botswana
Mozambique
Madagascar
South Africa
Swaziland
Lesotho

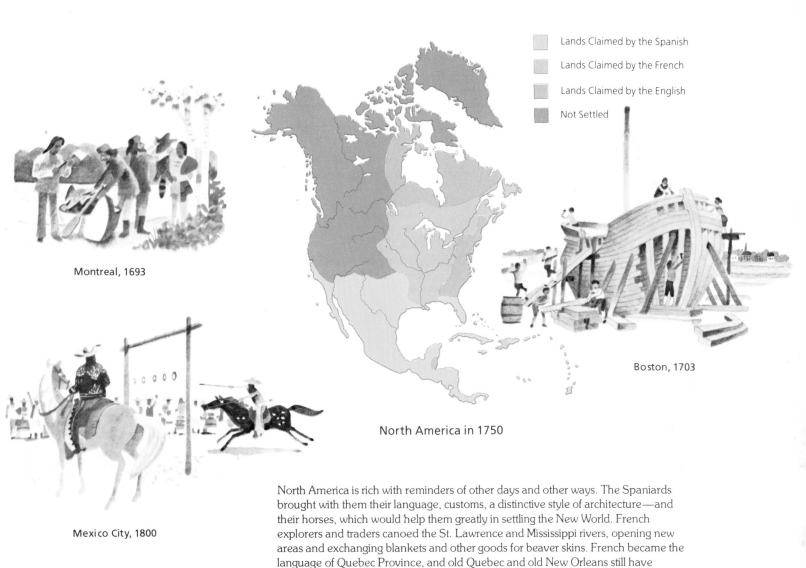

Montreal, 1693

Mexico City, 1800

North America in 1750

Lands Claimed by the Spanish

Lands Claimed by the French

Lands Claimed by the English

Not Settled

Boston, 1703

North America is rich with reminders of other days and other ways. The Spaniards brought with them their language, customs, a distinctive style of architecture—and their horses, which would help them greatly in settling the New World. French explorers and traders canoed the St. Lawrence and Mississippi rivers, opening new areas and exchanging blankets and other goods for beaver skins. French became the language of Quebec Province, and old Quebec and old New Orleans still have the look of French cities. British seamanship and shipbuilding skills helped make the English colonies, and later the U.S., a major trading power. English became the language of the U.S. and most of Canada.

Middle East as their colonies. Now all the countries are independent. Yet border disagreements continue. Particularly difficult is the establishment of a permanent boundary for Israel.

Many parts of southern Asia are also struggling with national borders. Pakistan and India have had constant disputes. And, within what was once part of Pakistan, people in a large piece of territory decided to form a new country. This new country is now known as Bangladesh.

Recent national—or political—changes have been widespread in Africa. Before World War II most of the continent was controlled by European nations. After 1950 nearly every colony that had been under European rule claimed independence—thus bringing

fifty-one new nations into the political world.

Even in North America, which seems so stable, the matter of borders is not completely settled. In Canada there are discussions about the position of French-speaking Quebec with regard to the rest of the nation, which is English-speaking.

The borders of the United States, itself, have not always been firm. France, Spain, Mexico, Sweden, the Netherlands, Great Britain, and even Russia have at one time claimed what are now parts of the country. Between 1861 and 1865 the violent Civil War was fought to prevent the southern states from making a new border to separate themselves from the northern states. And in just the recent past, the United States

has expanded to include Alaska and Hawaii as states.

National borders are constantly changing somewhere on the globe. Apparently this will always be so. It must be our goal to make the changes by peaceful, rather than by warlike, means.

The World's Nations	
Continent	Independent Nations
Africa	55
Asia	40
Europe	35
North America	27
South America	12
Australia and Oceania	14
Antarctica	0
TOTAL:	183

(Europe includes Soviet Union, and Asia includes Turkey.)

The Earth's Detectives

The research chemist studies the elements and how atoms combine and recombine into the variety of things on earth.

Learning about the earth is like being a detective. Thousands of men and women scientists around the world constantly devote their days—and often their nights—to probing the mysteries of the earth.

These detective-scientists are on survey ships that churn through sunny tropic seas or past threatening icebergs that glint in the starlight. They scramble over lava rocks to the lips of volcanoes that sputter and steam beneath them. They soar through the atmosphere photographing and later making maps of the land below. They peer through massive telescopes hoping to find answers to the questions of the earth's origin—and its future—in the wondrous reaches of deep space.

A tremendous array of instruments aids the scientists in their research. Some instruments measure the intensity and exact location of earthquakes. Other machines map the ocean's mountains, plains, and awesome trenches. And unmanned satellites scan the earth's surface.

Facts and figures obtained from these studies around the world are fed into computers. The computers organize the information and give it back to the scientists who use it in various ways. They check facts and scientific ideas, develop new scientific ideas, and in doing so help us better understand our earth.

Earth-scientists are detectives of the highest order. Theirs is a life of exciting research that helps all humanity.

The meteorologist understands the atmosphere and all its workings.

The volcanologist specializes in anything having to do with volcanoes.

Geophysicists study the earth and its atmosphere. Most of these scientists specialize in one field or another.

The seismologist investigates earthquakes.

The geologist examines the earth's crust for clues to the planet's past, present, and future.

The oceanographer explores the oceans, the tides and currents, the makeup of the waters, and the ocean beds.

MAPS, MAPS, MAPS

Its boiling core and its solid crust, its waters, atmosphere, plants and animals—these make up our ever-changing earth. Parts of it in time will grow warmer or cooler, wetter or drier. Living things will adapt or disappear and others will take their place. Mountains will poke their noses upward, then stop rising and be worn away by weather. Slowly, slowly, the continents will move, shift, change. A million years from now they will differ greatly from their present form. For now, let's look at maps of the continents as they are today.

Many kinds of maps are possible in an atlas. Here there are four for each of the continents except Antarctica. A *terrain* map shows mountains, waters, and plains. Another map shows how people have divided the continents into *countries*. *Life on the Land* maps picture people's use of the land. *Animal* maps show each of the continent's wildlife.

Turn now to the seven continents as we know them.

Europe/Terrain

Many parts of Europe lie under the shadows of towering mountains. The most splendid of these peaks are the Alps. These shining pyramids of snow and stone are found in Switzerland, southeastern France, Austria, southern Germany, northern Italy, and northern Yugoslavia. The Alps make these countries a sightseer's paradise in summer and a skier's adventureland in winter.

Three major mountain systems flow out of the central mass of the Alps like tails from a kite. One of these tails, the Apennines, reaches south into the boot of Italy. Another, the Dinaric Alps, makes a jagged trail through Yugoslavia and Albania into Greece. The third, the Carpathians, forms a graceful half-moon through Czechoslovakia and Romania.

Also reaching out from the Alps are many hills and plateaus. Nearly all of southern and central France is a wide upland, the Massif Central, that has been cut by rivers into hills. More hills ruffle parts of northern France and eastern Belgium—they are called the Ardennes Mountains, site of many fierce battles throughout history. Similar low hills and plateaus lie across southern Germany, in parts of Czechoslovakia, and in Austria.

Across the English Channel, Great Britain has a bumpy backbone known as the Pennine Chain of mountains. North of them are the famed Scottish Highlands, where long hills covered with purple-flowered heather roll like frozen ocean waves across the countryside.

Europe Facts

Sixth largest continent
Second in population: 673,900,000
64 cities over 1 million population
Highest mountain: Elbrus, 18,510 feet
 (5,642 meters)
Most densely populated continent:
 175 people per square mile (68 people
 per square kilometer)

Northern mainland Europe is marked by mountains of another kind. The uplands of Norway and Sweden are bleak and barren, especially as they approach the white magnificence of the Arctic Circle. Huge glaciers once rumbled over the landscape, clawing deep grooves into the mountains. These grooves, flooded by the ocean, have become long waterways called fjords. The fjords attract many tourists because of their awesome beauty.

Far to the east the Soviet Union's Ural Mountains mark the division between Europe and Asia. Such a mountain chain in the middle of a thousand-mile flatland is most unusual. The Urals are very old—formed about 225 million years ago. In that time they have worn down more and more.

Today the tallest of the Urals stands only a little more than six thousand feet (1,828.2 meters) above sea level, quite low in comparison to other major mountains.

Some of the most famous rivers in the world flow from Europe's mountains. Perhaps the best known is the Rhine, which rises in Switzerland and flows north past grape-clothed bluffs in Germany and France where the castles of medieval barons still scowl down on the river. Far longer than the Rhine is the fabled Danube River. It rises in Germany and drifts lazily in a southeasterly direction through seven nations and three capital cities before emptying into the Black Sea.

The north-central part of the continent is made up of the Great Northern European Plain. The huge region's rich farmlands supply food for much of Europe, and its many ores help to make the Ruhr Valley on the Rhine a world center for heavy industry. Food and machinery move out to the rest of Europe on a network of rivers connected by canals. The canals were dug by hand long ago in spillways, the natural trenches that were formed by the melting of the glacier twenty-five thousand years ago.

The Great Northern European Plain stretches from western France to nearly a thousand miles (1,609.3 kilometers) beyond Moscow, where it is broken at last by the rounded Urals. Here bustling Europe ends amid the lonely sweep of the wind through mountain forests.

The Scottish Highlands are so rough and rugged that many people live instead on the lower coastal plains. There the land is more easily farmed.

The coasts of Norway and Sweden were formed by glaciers pushing into the sea. When the ice melted, the sea filled the winding fingers, or fjords. Some fjords are nearly 4,000 feet (1,219.2 kilometers) deep.

spian Sea

Mykonos, at left, and the other Greek islands in the Aegean Sea are part of the Pindus Mountains of Greece. Millions of years ago the sea rose until only the tops of the mountains remained above the waters.

Europe/Countries and Cities

In some ways Europe looks more like a jigsaw puzzle than a reasonable grouping of thirty-five nations. The boundaries of those countries—from the huge Soviet Union to tiny Luxembourg—were agreed upon only after much haggling through the centuries. In recent times, World Wars I and II caused boundary changes, and several new nations were formed as well.

The borders of most countries stop at mountains, rivers, or seas. When the first tribes migrated into an area, they usually chose a homeland that had some natural barrier where their warriors could defend them from attack. Today, many countries still are edged by such natural borders.

Cities tell us much about peoples of the past. Rome and Athens were known thousands of years ago, and the Roman Forum and Colosseum and the Acropolis and statues of Athens hint at life in ancient times. Paris dates back more than two thousand years. It was founded around 52 B.C. by Roman

soldiers. Trondheim, in Norway, had its beginning around A.D. 998. Today it is the third largest city in Norway and an important export center. Clues in these and other cities hint at governments, religions, and pastimes of the people who once lived there.

The European continent averages 173 persons per square mile. Some of its countries, especially in the west, are among the most densely packed in the world. The Netherlands has 892 persons per square mile. But it is doing something few other countries are able to do—it is growing by reclaiming land from the sea.

Something a traveler moving through Europe notices is its many languages. Of the several dozen spoken, nearly all fall into three main groups.

The French, Italians, Spanish, Portuguese, and Romanians cannot understand one another. Nevertheless, all of their languages are based on the ancient Latin spoken by the Romans who once conquered those lands. These are the "Romance" languages.

The people of Germany, the Netherlands, England, Denmark, Sweden, and Norway speak six separate languages. Yet these, too, have their roots in a single language—the German of

About 2,300 years ago, Rome was the heart of Europe. Still standing are parts of the Roman Forum, which was both a marketplace and a meeting place for Roman citizens. The great pillars of the Forum buildings stood for the strength of the Roman Empire, which ruled over 50 million people on three continents.

the tribes which occupied those areas in ages past.

To the east, the peoples of Poland, Czechoslovakia, Yugoslavia, Bulgaria, and Russia all speak languages based on the Slavic language of tribes that once lived there.

You might ask why an Italian doesn't understand a Spaniard, since their languages are alike. Or why the Germanic-speaking Dane doesn't understand the Germanic-speaking Briton. The answer lies in terrain, distance, and culture. Peoples of neighboring lands often were cut off from each other by natural barriers, or were separated by too many miles to meet often and talk. The Pyrenees closed Spain from France. A branch of the Alps shut off France from Italy. The North Sea separated the English from the Danes. And vast differences in

cultures—life-styles—divided the Slavic-speaking Poles and the Russians. Each nation developed—over long ages—different ways of speaking what were once the same languages. In time the German of Germany was slightly different from that of the Netherlands. Across the North Sea the English people developed a distinct language using many German words, but also including words from Latin. And in the north, the Danes, Swedes, and Norwegians all used their own versions of the ancient German.

Today European languages are called Romance, Germanic, and Slavic. Only three major European countries do not fall into these groupings: Finland, Hungary, and Greece.

Each of the thirty-five nations of Europe has its own kind of government and a way of life that is unique to itself.

Europe/Life on the Land

Fishing

Hydrothermal Plant

Reindeer Herding

Coal Mining

Lumbering

Agricultural Area

Fishing

Canneries

Papermaking

Dairyland

Fishing

Offshore Oil Drilling

Cheese Making

Dairyland

Troika
(3-horse Sleigh)

Agricultural Area

Agricultural Area

Farming

Heavy Industry

Houses of Parliament

Heavy Industry (Steel)

Bulb Farming

Grimm's Fairy Tale
Country

Eiffel Tower

Oil Fields

Dairyland

Vineyards

Citrus Groves

Export by Sea

Matterhorn

Wheatlands

Light
Industry

Sheep Raised

Cork Harvesting

Water Sports

Roman Ruins

Olive Orchards

Bullfighting

Opera

Olive Orchards

Vineyards

Vineyards

Ancient Greek Ruins

Fishing

42

Lumbering

Fur Trapping

Oil Fields

Sawmills

Lumbering

Ballet

Oil Fields

St. Basil's

Wheatlands

Agricultural Area

Coal Mining

Fishing

Agricultural Area

Smelting of Ore

Oil Fields

Caviar Exported

Agricultural Area

Cotton

Fishing

Europe is actually a long, rather narrow "arm" of land that sticks westward out of Asia into the sea. No part of western Europe is more than 300 miles (482.79 kilometers) from the sea, and the whole continent has a ragged coastline with "fingers" of the sea reaching in everywhere, and with thousands of islands of all sizes close by. Thus, for a great many of the people of Europe the sea is right at their doorstep and plays a tremendously important part in their lives. Tens of thousands of Europeans fish for a living or work as sailors on merchant ships.

On the mountains and lowlands of Norway, Sweden, and Finland are vast evergreen forests that supply lumber for furniture and building and wood pulp for paper. Vineyards in the rolling, hilly regions of France and Germany, and farther south in Italy and Spain, produce huge amounts of fine wine that is sent throughout the world. Olive orchards in Spain and Italy also provide the world's major olive crop.

Between the highland areas, on the great plain that sweeps from the Soviet Union to France, growing narrower all the way, lie most of Europe's farms, where bigger crops of potatoes, wheat, barley, oats, rye, and sugar beets are produced than anywhere else in the world. More than half the land in Europe is used for farming, and about one-fourth of all Europeans farm.

However, modern industry—mining and manufacturing—began in Europe, so Europe abounds with busily humming industrial areas and has long been the leading continent for world trade and industry. The Soviet Union is the world's second ranking manufacturing nation, after the United States. West Germany ranks third. And Japan, France, Great Britain, Italy, Canada, and East Germany are fourth, fifth, sixth, seventh, eighth, and ninth, respectively.

Europe has less land area than any other continent except Australia, but it has more people than any other continent except huge Asia. Thus, the people of Europe are often packed quite closely together. Yet, in the recent past, people of European nations right next to one another often had very different ways and customs and even wore different kinds of clothing. Today, except for differences in language, most European people are much more alike.

Europe/Its Animals

Skua

Herring

Barnacle Goose

Reindeer

Grey Seal

Wolverine

Lemming

Hare

Red Deer

Basking Shark

Otter

Black Grouse

Pheasant

Badger

Hedgehog

Atlantic Salmon

Rabbit

Fox

Chamois

Moorhen

Red-legged Partridge

Stork

Marmot

Squirrel

Great Bustard

Barbary Ape

Sole

Ferruginous Duck

Hoopoe

Spanish Mackerel

Most of the vast, animal-filled forests that once covered much of Europe were cut down long ago to make room for farms, cities, and towns. Many of Europe's animals were hunted for centuries, until they were wiped out. But in a few wild places still left—national parks, game preserves, and a few out-of-the-way places—some of the animals that once abounded in Europe can still be found.

A few of the shaggy, tusked boars that were the favorite game animal of medieval nobles still root in the underbrush of small forests in central Europe. Packs of wolves still howl in some places, and in the northern Soviet Union brown bears still lumber about. In the north of Sweden, Norway, Finland, and the western Soviet Union reindeer are herded like cattle by people of the northland, the Lapps.

In the Pyrenees Mountains between France and Spain lives the Pyrenean ibex, a mountain goat with gracefully curled horns. Another kind of mountain goat, the chamois, is found in the Alps.

Europe also has numerous small animals. Foxes, badgers, moles, rabbits, and squirrels are found in many places. Little, plump lemmings abound in the mountains of Norway and Sweden. The hedgehog is common in northern Europe and especially well-known in England. It has short, sharp "spikes" all over its back, like the quills of a porcupine only much thicker.

Small, striped wildcats prowl in parts of Yugoslavia and Bulgaria, and a rather large wildcat, the Spanish lynx, lives in Spain. It is three feet (0.91 meter) long with pointed, tufted ears and thick whiskers—a fast, fierce hunter.

Sparrows, thrushes, finches, nightingales, and ravens are found throughout central Europe. So are large birds of prey such as falcons and eagles. During the summer the big white stork is a common sight in cities of the Netherlands, Belgium, and Germany, where it nests on the chimneys of houses.

Various kinds of lizards and snakes, tortoises and turtles, frogs, toads, and salamanders are found in woodlands and meadows throughout Europe. Trout, salmon, and other fish swim in clear streams above the polluted areas. Many of the animal species found in Europe are also found on the North American continent.

In a protected forest of Poland about 1,600 wisents, the bisons of prehistoric Europe; live as they did many thousands of years ago—feeding in grassy clearings. Full grown, the animals stand six feet (1.82 meters) high at the shoulder.

Raven

Whimbrel

Brown Bear

Pine Marten

Wild Boar

Wolf

Griffon Vulture

Roe Deer

Lesser Spotted Eagle

Tur

Octopus

Conger Eel

Africa/Terrain

One of the world's great natural wonders is Victoria Falls, on the Zambezi River in southern Africa. They are over a mile (1.6 kilometers) long and with a drop of nearly 400 feet (122 meters)—wider and higher than Niagara Falls.

Africa, the second largest continent, is really a gigantic plateau which stands mostly one thousand feet (304.8 meters) above sea level. It is mostly lower in the north and west and higher in the east and south. On all sides the edges of this great tablelike landmass drop off abruptly to the surrounding oceans and seas. A few narrow coastal plains are to be found—such as those along Ghana, Nigeria, and the Ivory Coast.

Four mighty rivers rise in the high interior. The Niger flows out of wild grasslands where lions roam. The Nile, longest of the world's rivers, drifts past temples built by long-dead Egyptian kings. The Congo drains a dark, humid rain forest. The Zambezi cuts across a vast, thorny woodland.

All of Africa's rivers contain impassable rapids and so are only partly open to boat traffic. For this reason, Africa's mineral and vegetable resources cannot readily be shipped to the cities. This is Africa's great misfortune.

Another problem for Africa's economic development is its smooth and regular coastline. For stretches of hundreds of miles there are no shelters for ships. Swampy coasts thick with stands of mangrove trees make access to the land difficult with their thick jumble of roots standing above the shore. Thus Africa has few good harbors around which a Rio de Janeiro or New York could develop.

Africa has some magnificent mountains. The Atlas Range is a major chain that rims the continent's northern edge for 1,500 miles (2,413.95 kilometers) through Morocco, Algeria, and Tunisia. It was formed at the same time as the European Alps. Both are the result of

Africa's Great Rift Valley cuts a north-south trench equal to one-sixth of the earth's circumference—a distance of 4,000 miles (6,437.2 kilometers). In places the valley is broken by plateaus and mountains, but it can be traced by the many lakes and seas which fill its long pockets. The cutaway at right shows some of those bodies of water.

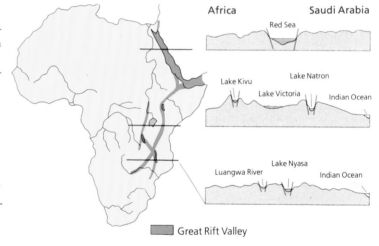

Great Rift Valley

the collision of Africa with Europe many millions of years ago. After the collision, Africa recoiled, or drifted, back south. The gap between the two continents filled with water to become the Mediterranean Sea.

In East Africa, the peaks of the Ruwenzori Range follow two nearly parallel north-south lines. Among the eastern mountains, snow-crested Mount Kilimanjaro soars to more than nineteen thousand feet (5,791.2 meters)—Africa's highest peak.

Between the high eastern ranges lies the mysterious Great Rift Valley. This is a long rip in the earth's surface where

the land dropped down more than a mile (1.6 kilometers). Several beautiful lakes nestle in this rift. Lying on the plateau between the two major branches of the rift is the largest, Lake Victoria, which is almost as big as Scotland.

The Drakensberg Mountains of South Africa are the most unusual range on the continent. As seen from a distance they appear to rise skyward from the earth. Actually, they are not true mountains, just tilted-up portions of the gigantic plateau which makes up Africa.

Few people outside Africa realize just

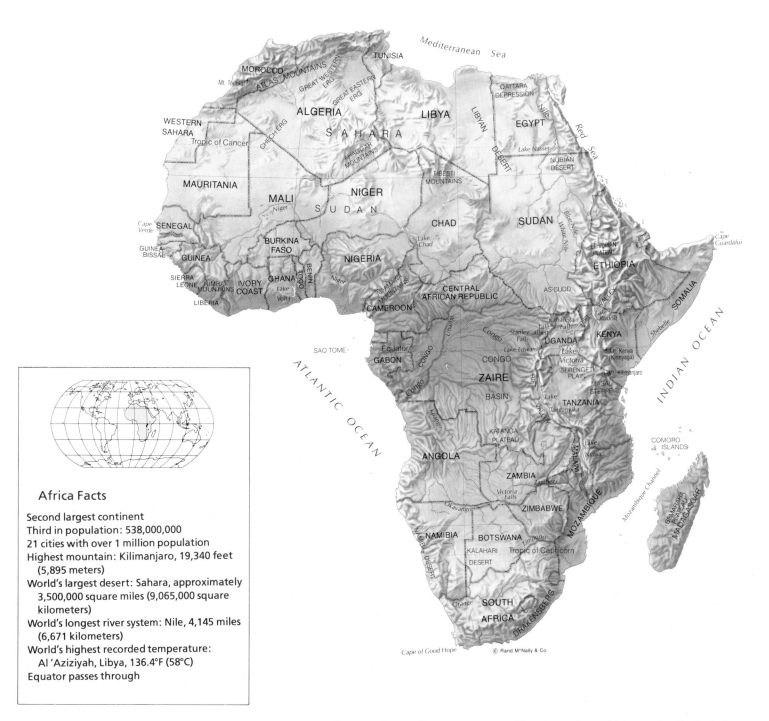

Mediterranean Sea

MOROCCO
Mt. Toubkal
ATLAS MOUNTAINS
GREAT WESTERN ERG
TUNISIA
GREAT EASTERN ERG
ALGERIA
LIBYA
LIBYAN DESERT
EGYPT
QATTARA DEPRESSION
Nile
Red Sea
WESTERN SAHARA
Tropic of Cancer
CHECH ERG
S A H A R A
AHAGGAR MOUNTAINS
TIBESTI MOUNTAINS
Lake Nasser
NUBIAN DESERT
MAURITANIA
MALI
Niger
NIGER
S U D A N
CHAD
Lake Chad
SUDAN
Blue Nile
White Nile
ETHIOPIAN PLATEAU
Cape Guardafui
Cape Verde
SENEGAL
BURKINA FASO
NIGERIA
ETHIOPIA
GUINEA BISSAU
GUINEA
SIERRA LEONE
NIMBA MOUNTAINS
IVORY COAST
GHANA
TOGO
BENIN
Niger
Lake Volta
ADAMAWA MOUNTAINS
CAMEROON
CENTRAL AFRICAN REPUBLIC
AS-SUDD
RIFT VALLEY
Lake Rudolf
SOMALIA
Shebelle
LIBERIA
SAO TOME
GABON
CONGO
Equator
CONGO
Congo
ZAIRE
BASIN
Congo
Ubangi
Stanley Falls
Kabalega Falls
Lake Albert
UGANDA
Lake Edward
Lake Victoria
SERENGETI PLAIN
Mt. Kenya (Kirinyaga)
KENYA
Mt. Kilimanjaro
MASAI STEPPE
INDIAN OCEAN
ATLANTIC OCEAN
Kwango
Kasai
TANZANIA
Lake Tanganyika
KATANGA PLATEAU
Lake Nyasa
MALAWI
COMORO ISLANDS
ANGOLA
ZAMBIA
Zambezi
Mozambique Channel
BENARIHA PLATEAU
MADAGASCAR
Victoria Falls
Okavango
ZIMBABWE
MOZAMBIQUE
NAMIBIA
BOTSWANA
Limpopo
Tropic of Capricorn
NAMIB DESERT
KALAHARI DESERT
Orange
SOUTH AFRICA
DRAKENSBERG
Cape of Good Hope
© Rand McNally & Co.

Africa Facts

Second largest continent
Third in population: 538,000,000
21 cities with over 1 million population
Highest mountain: Kilimanjaro, 19,340 feet
(5,895 meters)
World's largest desert: Sahara, approximately
3,500,000 square miles (9,065,000 square
kilometers)
World's longest river system: Nile, 4,145 miles
(6,671 kilometers)
World's highest recorded temperature:
Al 'Aziziyah, Libya, 136.4°F (58°C)
Equator passes through

Great, windswept deserts cover most of Egypt, a northeast African nation that includes the Sinai Peninsula. Yet, people have learned to live in these dry places.

how huge the continent is. More than a hundred Great Britains could be deposited within Africa's borders and there would still be more than enough room for five Frances and four West Germanys. The entire United States could be placed in just the Sahara Desert, which extends for 3,200 sandy miles (5,149.76 kilometers) across northern Africa.

Yet despite its great size, Africa is largely undeveloped. To tap the resources locked within the continent remains a great challenge for its people and for the more prosperous nations which wish to invest in Africa's future.

Africa/Countries and Cities

Africa today has fifty-five countries. In talking about them, the countries are generally grouped in five large areas: North Africa, West Africa, central Africa, South Africa, and East Africa. The countries in each area have some things in common.

Civilization has a long history in North Africa. Egypt was the site of one of our very first cultures. Later the ancient city of Carthage, in present-day Tunisia, was the center of a powerful state that for a time rivaled even mighty Rome.

During the seventh century A.D. the religion of Islam—the followers of which are called Muslims—was adopted by most North African nations. Beautiful Muslim mosques were built in what is now Libya, Algeria,

Tunisia, and Morocco. Islam is still the religion of North Africa's people.

Contact between the North Africans and the Africans to the south was made difficult by the sandy and rocky wastes of the Sahara. This desert extends south from the Atlas Mountains and the Mediterranean Sea for nearly 1,500 sunbaked miles (2,413.95 kilometers). Caravans did manage to open a few routes across the desert, and there was some trading for goods and slaves.

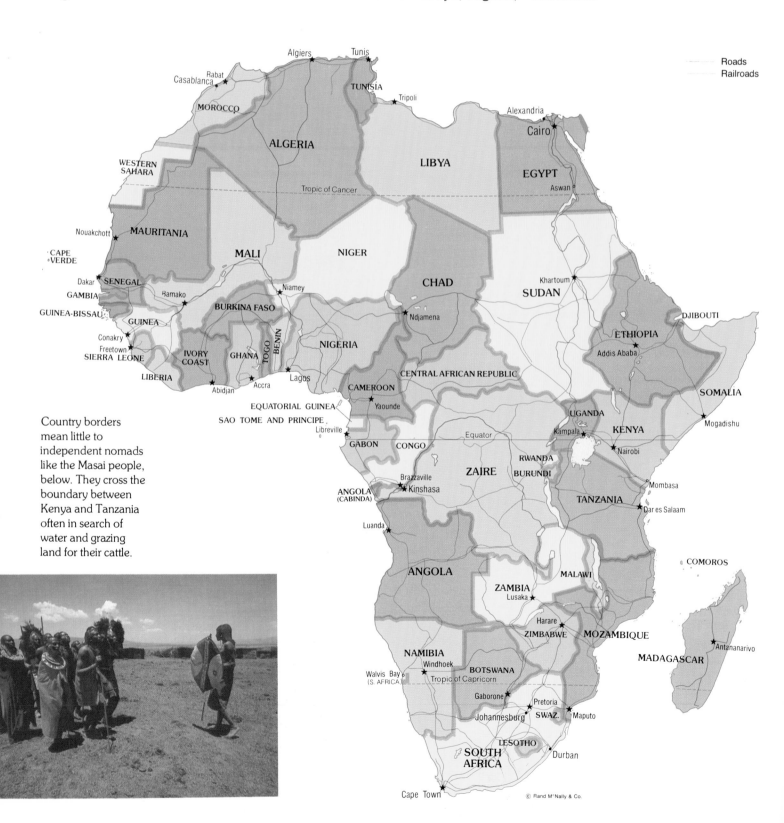

Country borders mean little to independent nomads like the Masai people, below. They cross the boundary between Kenya and Tanzania often in search of water and grazing land for their cattle.

Roads
Railroads

© Rand McNally & Co.

Throughout history North Africa has been distinct from the rest of Africa. Most North Africans are white and speak the Semitic language which in several forms is also spoken by the Jewish and Arabian peoples. Almost one-fifth of all the people in Africa live in the countries of North Africa.

West Africa, much of which is a moist, hot lowland area bordering the Atlantic Ocean, was long known as the slave coast. Through the centuries raiders visited these shores, kidnapped the people, carried them away in ships, and sold them as laborers in many parts of the world. Bitter tales of families torn apart, misery, death, and loss of human dignity are still remembered from this terrible period in Africa's history.

Today, more than one-fourth of the people in Africa live in these countries which border the Atlantic. Nigeria, with over 89 million people, is Africa's most populous nation. Ghana, too, is quite heavily settled along the western coast.

The equator passes through the continent's third area, central Africa. The most important nation here is Zaire, with over 32 million people. The Congo River and the rivers that feed into it are almost completely contained within Zaire, and the country is almost smothered by a rain forest. The climate is steamy, and insects are not only a nuisance but a hazard to good health.

Eastern Africa is like another world, compared to the rest of the continent. Its western border is marked by mountains which soar above the Great Rift Valley. The climate is far drier than in neighboring Zaire.

The people of Tanzania, Kenya, and Uganda live mainly in these uplands, particularly around the deep water of Lake Tanganyika and the huge expanse of Lake Victoria. Farther north, in Ethiopia, most of the population clusters on the Ethiopian Plateau.

The continent's fifth area, southern Africa, lies mostly outside the hot regions of the equator. The Republic of South Africa boasts some of the most fertile land on the continent and a climate rather like Europe's. For this reason the land appealed to Europeans. The British and the Dutch fought for it. Even though the British army won, the

Though many Africans still cling to their old ways of life, modern cities have sprung up across the continent. Nairobi, Kenya, is one such teeming center.

Women carry their wares to market as their ancestors did before them. Colorful cotton cloth has been made in the West African country of Nigeria for centuries.

Dutch, known as Boers, stayed on in large numbers. It was the Boers who farmed the rich land and founded successful businesses. Out of a population of over 29 million, four and a half million Europeans control the country.

Europeans also settled the area they named Rhodesia. Rhodesia's black peoples, which make up more than 94 percent of the population, recently took control of the government. They renamed the country Zimbabwe. There

has been much political strife in this country.

The fifty-five countries which make up Africa are as different from one another as the lofty mountains of the Great Rift are from rain forests found on the equator. The people of Africa have only begun to control their governments in the past thirty or so years. The countries have only begun to grow. We can only guess where that growth will take Africa.

Africa/Life on the Land

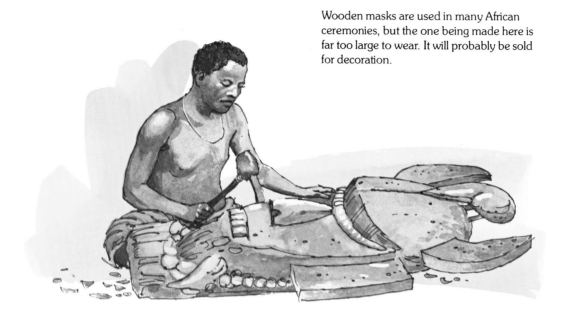

Wooden masks are used in many African ceremonies, but the one being made here is far too large to wear. It will probably be sold for decoration.

Agricultural Area

Peanuts

Chocolate

Most Africans are either farmers or herders. Many African farmers use old-fashioned farming methods, but some have begun to use modern machinery, such as tractors.

Little farming can be done in the hot, dry northern part of the continent. In a narrow strip of land that runs along the coasts of Morocco, Algeria, and Tunisia farmers can grow grapes, olives, lemons and oranges, nuts, and a few grains. About half the people of Egypt work farmlands along the banks of the Nile River, mainly growing cotton. But in most of North Africa, people can only make a living by traveling with small flocks of sheep from one area of sparse grass to another. Except for cotton, not much of what is produced in North Africa is of importance to the rest of the world.

However, some important crops are grown in West Africa. Cacao beans, from which chocolate and cocoa are made, come from here, together with palm nuts, used for making soap and cosmetics. Much of the world's chocolate and palm oil come from Africa. Rubber is also exported from West Africa,

Rubber and palm nuts are also produced in central Africa, where the great rain forest spreads. In this area, many people live as their ancestors did for

thousands of years, in tiny villages, practicing a very primitive kind of farming. And here are found the little people known as Pygmies, who still live mainly by hunting.

In large parts of East Africa, too, people live much as they always have. But here the main way of life is the herding of cattle. However, along a narrow strip of the coast a very important crop, sisal, is grown. Much of the rope used everywhere in the world is made from sisal leaf fibers.

The Kalahari Desert covers thousands of square miles of South Africa and is the home of some of the world's last Stone Age people, the so-called Bushmen, who move about, hunting and gathering whatever plant food they can find. But farther south, the land proved fertile for farming and grazing for the Dutch farmers and cattle raisers who settled there. Wheat and corn are grown in vast areas, and large amounts of livestock are raised.

South Africa is also rich in minerals. Most of the world's diamonds come from the famous Kimberley mines, and gold is mined in the Witwatersrand district. High quality iron and coal are also mined and made into steel. However, outside of South Africa, very little manufacturing is done in Africa, even in the large cities.

Every land has its folklore. A famous African tale tells of Ananse the Spider Man who tried to keep all the wisdom in the world for himself by stuffing it in a large pot. But the pot fell as Ananse tried to hide it in a tree, and all the wisdom blew away. And that, says the story, is how wisdom was spread throughout the world.

Moorish-style Architecture

Agricultural Area

Corn

Wheat

Vineyards

Olives

Fishing

Cairo

Sphinx

Nomad with Goats

Oil Fields

Tobacco

The Great Pyramid at Giza

Dates Harvested

Goods Shipped by Caravan

Sand Dunes

Cotton Grown

Cotton Made into Cloth

Leather Products Made

African Village

Sheep Raised

Rubber

Palm Oil

Mining

Cattle Raised

Plantains (African Bananas)

Tourists Welcomed

Cattle Raised

Cacao Beans (Chocolate)

Central Forests

Copra (Dried Coconut) Shipped

Oil Fields

Pygmy

Mt. Kilimanjaro

Minerals Mined

Agricultural Area

Coal Mines

Masai Tribesman

Corn

Tea

Diamond Mines

Victoria Falls

Citrus Fruits

Sheep Raised

Yams

Vanilla Beans Grown

Gold Mines

51

Africa/Its Animals

Africa is a continent of great forests, great grassy plains, and great deserts. Each of these different landscapes has its own special animals.

In the north the enormous Sahara Desert spreads across thousands of miles. Not many animals live in that hot wasteland, and those that do are able to survive with little or no water. In places where scrubby plants grow there are a few small herds of addax, a kind of little antelope with tall, twisted horns. An addax never drinks. It gets the moisture it needs from the plants it eats. The jerboa, a mouselike creature with long hind legs and a long, tufted tail, sleeps in a hole in the sand by day and comes out in the cool night to feed on plants and insects. Jerboas and other little animals and birds are hunted by the fennec, a big-eared, desert fox.

Of course, the best-known animal of the Sahara is the one-humped Arabian camel, also known as the dromedary. But these animals have actually lived in the Sahara for only about two thousand years. They were brought here from the Middle East. All the camels in the Sahara are used as tame beasts of burden.

Across the middle of Africa is a great rain forest. This is the home of the chimpanzee which moves about in small bands living mainly on fruit and tender, young plants. The rain forest is also the home of the big, burly gorilla, actually a shy and gentle creature. Here, too, are found buffalo, leopards, many kinds of monkeys, and the little okapi, a brown-bodied animal with white-striped legs. It resembles a horse, but is related to the giraffe. In swamps and rivers that lie in the forest area crocodiles swim in search of prey, and bulky hippopotamuses munch on water plants.

Vast, grassy plains lie between the Sahara and the rain forest, and south of the forest as well. Herds of zebra, eland, and gnu, or wildebeest, graze on these plains. Giraffes browse among clusters of trees. Rhinoceroses trot to water holes to wallow in the mud after feeding. Herds of African elephants, the largest of all land animals, plod on their way. Here, too, the spotted cheetah, swiftest of all animals, runs down its prey. And here is heard the shattering roar of the powerful African lion, king of all the beasts.

Tarpon
Addax
Fennec
Pangolin
Colobus Monkey

Despite their fearful appearance, gorillas are generally gentle beasts who eat only plants. They will harm people only if bothered or attacked.

Jackal

Dromedary

Crowned
Crane

Eared
Vulture

Dorcas Gazelle

Barbary Sheep

Striped Hyena

Crocodile

Greater
Kudu

Giraffe

Aardvark

Elephant

Baboon

Chimpanzee

Gorilla

Black Rhinoceros

Leopard

Hornbill

White
Pelican

Cape Buffalo

Hippopotamus

Zebra

Lion

Tenrec

Eland

Chameleon

Python

Wildebeest

Ring-tailed
Lemur

Cheetah

Impala

Angelfish

Ostrich

Sacred Ibis

Asia/Terrain

Asia covers more area than North America, Europe, and Australia combined. Great numbers of people struggle for a living in Asia—nearly three billion, more people than live in all the rest of the world! Yet because Asia is so big, there are places where an eagle could fly for hours, even days, and never see a human being.

The empty, and nearly empty, parts of Asia take up more space than parts of the continent where people live. For example, the area of the Soviet Union known as Siberia reaches eastward from the Ural Mountains, where Asia begins, for more than three thousand long, lonely miles (4,827.9 kilometers) to the Pacific Ocean. It is a vast region of cold winds and frosty earth.

To the south of Siberia is an equally large, equally harsh region. A desert blots out most life across central Asia. This desert begins in the blowing sand dunes of Saudi Arabia, sweeps across much of Jordan, Iraq, and Iran, and continues through the southern Soviet Union. It blisters Mongolia, where it ends as the forbidding Gobi Desert.

The great Asian desert is bounded on the south by the highest mountain ranges in the world. Highest of all are the Himalayas. Mount Everest, in the Himalayas, reaches five and a half miles (8.85 kilometers) into air so thin that climbers must wear oxygen masks to stay alive.

South of the Himalayas lies a warm, wet triangle of land, the subcontinent of India. Some of the most important areas in India and Bangladesh are around the Ganges and Brahmaputra rivers. This is the agricultural core of the land. Jute, rice, wheat, and sugarcane are grown here.

Summer monsoons—rain-bearing winds—sweep across India from June to September. The monsoons blow from the southwest, across the Indian Ocean, picking up moisture and carrying rain to India and part of Pakistan. The monsoons make the difference between good and bad crops. Since the winds do not reach far into Pakistan, some of the people there must irrigate their land. They rely on water from the Indus River, which rises in Tibet north of the Himalayas and flows through Pakistan.

That part of Asia called the Far East includes three of the most heavily populated countries in the world: China, Japan, and Korea

For thousands of years, China was cut off from other countries. Frigid Siberia and the bleak Gobi Desert separated China from Europe. The plateau of Tibet, three miles (4.82 kilometers) high, and the Himalayas beyond were a barrier between China and India. With the growth of seamanship in the West, China began to trade with other countries.

China's climate is cool in the north, warm and wet in the south. This makes a difference in the kind of food grown in the areas—wheat in the north, rice in the south.

China has three major rivers. In the north is the Hwang Ho (Yellow) River. The Yangtze is in the south, so is the Hsi. People have settled heavily along these rivers.

Japan was once cut off from its neighbors, too. The Pacific Ocean made trade difficult. China was more than 400 miles (643.72 kilometers) away and Korea was 100 miles (160.93 kilometers) away.

The four main Japanese islands are part of a chain of rather recently formed volcanic mountains. Much of the land is covered with volcanic ash and lava which once spouted from such mighty cones as Mount Fuji. Japan still feels the effects of its volcanic birth. The land somewhere in

Farmers grow rice on the hilly terrain of Nepal by planting their crops in terraced fields. Beyond loom the Himalayas, the highest mountains in the world.

Israel's Negev Desert blooms with the help of water pumped from the Sea of Galilee.

Asia Facts

Largest continent
First in population: 2,946,200,000
101 cities with over 1 million population
World's highest mountain: Everest,
    29,028 feet (8,848 meters)
World's largest "lake": Caspian Sea, 143,240
    square miles (370,990 square kilometers)
World's lowest inland point: Dead Sea, 1,312
    feet (400 meters) below sea level

Japan shakes with an earthquake on the average of four times a day.

South of China is the area known as Southeast Asia. It includes Indochina, the Malay Peninsula, and the islands of Indonesia. The region is a gigantic rain forest, and the air is steamy. There are a few fertile river valleys—the Mekong, which passes through nearly all of Indochina; the Menam in Thailand; and the Irrawaddy in Burma.

In Indonesia, near the equator, the climate becomes even hotter. These islands are part of a mountain chain which is mostly hidden under the sea. The dark trees, thick undergrowth, and looping vines of dripping rain forests cover all the islands except Java.

Asia is a vast continent. It has some of the world's highest mountains, longest rivers, largest deserts, and coldest and hottest climates.

Asia/Countries and Cities

Because Asia is so large, its countries have tended to form in clusters. The continent has five big groupings of nations. The first borders the eastern edge of the continent and came to be called the Far East. China and Japan are the leading countries in the Far East. Indochina and the islands of Indonesia make up the second group. The third group formed on or near the southern triangle of land which contains India. The desert countries occupy the fourth area. Siberia, a part of the Soviet Union, stands alone in the fifth.

China has the most people of any country in the world—over one billion. One of every five persons on earth is Chinese!

For endless centuries China was the most powerful nation in the Far East. Then the Industrial Revolution occurred in Europe. Goods and arms were manufactured in great numbers. Suddenly Great Britain, France, and other Western nations had military power. China's growing weakness became clear after the British won the so-called Opium War of 1839-1842. Today, under Communist leadership, China is trying to regain its military and industrial strength.

The industrial giant of Asia is Japan. When Commodore Perry opened Japan to foreign trade in 1853, the Japanese began to adopt Western ways of manufacturing. Today they are fourth only to the United States, Soviet Union and West Germany, in industrial muscle.

For centuries Korea was caught between the two big Eastern powers. Both China and Japan had ruled the country. After World War II Korea was once more trapped in battle, with the result that the country is now split. The 16 million people of Communist North Korea look to the Soviet Union as their ally. Anti-Communist South Korea, with 36 million people, looks to the Western nations.

The countries of Indochina, the second Asian group, are also somewhat influenced, culturally, by the Chinese. Indeed, the very word *Vietnam* is

Built to keep out invading Mongols, the Great Wall of China winds for some 1,500 mountainous miles (2,414 kilometers). It is actually visible from the moon.

Chinese for "far south." Except for the Malay Peninsula at the southern tip, the nations of Indochina formed around river valleys where food grows well. Burma formed around the Irrawaddy River, and Thailand around the Menam. Kampuchea (formerly Cambodia) and Vietnam share the lower end of the Mekong River, while Laos grew around a higher part.

Over 153 million people live in Indonesia, making it among the five most populated countries on earth. The Indonesians are scattered over many of the 13,667 islands. They speak a number of languages and have a rather low standard of living. As a result, Indonesia's influence in world affairs is not as great as its population would suggest.

The third grouping of countries is contained on or near the Indian subcontinent. These are India, Pakistan, Bangladesh, and Sri Lanka. All these nations struggle with poverty. India is second only to China as the world's most populated country. Its over 669 million people live in overcrowded cities and villages. In neighboring Bangladesh fewer than ten percent of the people live in cities. The land is fertile, but farming methods are so poor that enough rice cannot be grown to feed the eighty-nine and a half million people of Bangladesh. Hunger visits this part of the world often.

The desert nations occupy the fourth area of Asia. People are fewer here than in other regions, for there is not enough water for large-scale farming. Turkey has more agricultural land than any other country in the region, but has just 46 million people. Only in Israel, established in 1948 as a Jewish homeland, does the population density—the number of people per square mile—reach that of the European countries.

The fifth area of Asia is Siberia, part of the Soviet Union. It has only a few people who live in widely separated communities. An important manufacturing center developed here after World War II in the Kuznetsk Basin. A third of the Soviet Union's coal comes from the region—as do farm machinery, chemicals, and building materials.

Civilization is old in Asia. Traditions of the many groups of people who live here had their beginnings in the very dawn of history.

Asia/Life on the Land

More than half the people in the world live in Asia, and about two-thirds of them make their living by farming. On many parts of the continent, farming is done by very old-fashioned methods, with no machinery and using only crude tools.

In much of China, Japan, India, and warm, wet Southeast Asia, rice is the most important crop. It is the main food of a great many Asian people, and Asia produces most of the world's rice. Most of the world's tea is produced in Japan, China, and India, and much of our natural rubber comes from Southeast Asia.

Cotton is the main crop of parts of Southwest Asia where farming can be done. Coffee, olives, grapes, dates, citrus fruits, and grains are also raised.

The land of northern Asia is too cold for much farming, and the highlands of central Asia are too poor for any crops. In the north, people do some herding of reindeer, cattle, and sheep, and the vast northern evergreen forests produce much lumber. In the central region some livestock herding is done. In particular, the karakul, or Persian lamb, is raised for its wool and hide. The wool is made into beautiful Oriental rugs and sent throughout the world.

Of course, nothing much can grow in the vast deserts of Southwest Asia. But far beneath the barren sands lie large amounts of oil. More than one-half of all the world's oil comes from this part of Asia.

There is only scattered industry in most of Southwest, Southeast, and central Asia. Only the nations of Israel, Japan, China, and the eastern Soviet Union have many factories and do much manufacturing. Japan is one of the leading manufacturers of automobiles and television sets in the world. Japan also has a large fishing industry.

A great many of the people of Asia are followers of the ancient Hindu religion. Many others are followers of the religion of Islam, and still others are Buddhists. Christianity is followed only in a few places. Thus, most of the holidays and customs throughout Asia are far different from those in Europe, North and South America, and Australia.

In a famous Arabian tale, a small boy named Aladdin finds an old lamp. He rubs it and a genie appears to do his bidding.

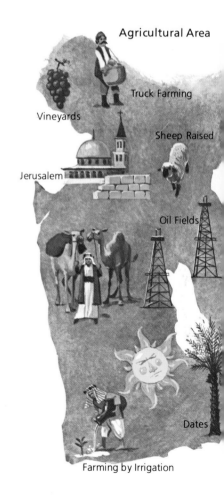

Agricultural Area

Truck Farming

Vineyards

Sheep Raised

Jerusalem

Oil Fields

Dates

Farming by Irrigation

The Indonesian island of Bali is famous for its folk dances. One, called the *legong,* tells an ancient story of love and battle. Each movement has a meaning and tells part of the story. Balinese girls practice for years to learn these complicated dances.

Mining

Fur Trapping

Logging

Truck Farming

Reindeer Herds

Mining

Smelting of Ore

Rice Grown

Cossack Dancer

Mining

Truck Farming

Logging

Light and Heavy Industry

Wheatlands

Wheatlands

Tea Grown

Great Wall of China

Hydroelectric Power

Steel Manufactured

Gate of Heavenly Peace

Citrus Fruits Grown

Sheep Raised

Smelting of Ore

Farming

Goods Shipped by Caravan

Traditional Chinese Urn

Chinese Junk

Ruins of Persepolis, Persia

Palace of the Dalai Lama

Agricultural Area

Agricultural Area

Corn

Cacao (Chocolate)

Persian Carpet

Wheat

Manufacturing

Mt. Everest

Cotton

Bathing in the Sacred Ganges

Coconuts

Taj Mahal

Burmese Temples

Fishing

Logging

Rice Grown

Tea Grown

Oil

Coconuts

Agricultural Area

Fishing

Rubber

Teak

Coffee

Asia/Its Animals

Asia, the giant of continents, spreads from far northern lands that are snow-covered nine months a year, to steamy, hot southern jungles. Thus, an enormous number of different kinds of animals are found here.

Most animals of northern Asia are like those in the far north of Europe—reindeer, foxes, hare, and tiny, mouselike lemmings. But in northern China and Korea prowls the thick-furred Siberian tiger, completely at home in cold and snow. The biggest of all cats, it is often as much as thirteen feet (3.96 meters) long.

Cold deserts lie in central Asia, and on them is found the shaggy, two-humped Bactrian camel. Some of these animals are still wild, but many are used as beasts of burden. The Bactrian camel's relative, the one-humped Arabian camel, or dromedary, is found on warmer deserts to the west.

Yaks, huge wild cattle five feet (1.52 meters) high at the shoulder and covered with long, thick fur, live in the high, cold land of Tibet. Many tame yaks are used as beasts of burden by the people of this part of central Asia.

The forests of southern Asia swarm with animals—monkeys, tree-dwelling clouded leopards, small herds of the wild cattle called gaurs, and a dwindling number of tigers. Indian elephants move through the forest in herds of from ten to fifty. Neither as big nor as fierce as African elephants, they are easily tamed, and many have been trained to work for people.

The deadly king cobra, the world's longest poisonous snake, whose bite can kill a human within fifteen minutes, also makes the forest its home. So does the cobra's mortal enemy—the fast, clever, weasellike mongoose which will attack and eat a cobra or any other snake on sight!

In forests on the islands of Borneo and Sumatra lives the red-furred great ape, the orangutan, which may be five feet (1.52 meters) tall. It lives in trees where it swings from branch to branch with its long arms.

And in bamboo forests in a part of Asia where China and Tibet come together lives the famous giant panda. Although it and its relative, the smaller red panda, resemble bears, they are not bears. They belong to a separate family of animals.

Imperial Eagle

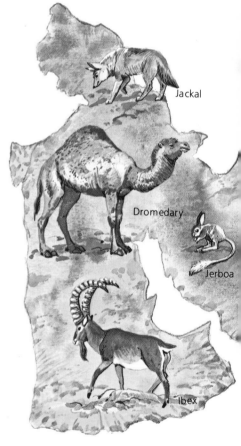

Jackal

Dromedary

Jerboa

Ibex

The largest horns grown by any wild animal are those of a sheep called the Pamir argali, or Marco Polo's argali. Marco Polo found this unusual creature during his travels across central Asia. The sheep's horns spiral outward and have been known to reach a record length of seventy-five inches (190.5 centimeters).

Polar Bear

Killer Whale

Arctic Fox

Willow Grouse

Sea Eagle

Elk

Snowy Owl

Wolf

Harbor Seal

Lynx

Przewalski's Horse

Raccoon-like Dog

Japanese Macaque

Saiga

Yak

Giant Panda

Bactrian Camel

Mandarin Duck

Japanese Crane

Snow Leopard

Pheasant

Water Buffalo

Dolphin

Tiger

Indian Elephant

Cormorant

Flyingfish

Macaque

Peafowl

Gibbon

Cobra

Orangutan

Mongoose

South America/Terrain

Almost in the clouds is Lake Titicaca, on a windswept plateau in the Andes. It is South America's largest lake—3,500 square miles (9,065 square kilometers)—and the highest large lake in the world.

Mountains span the length of South America like a gigantic, rocky backbone. Though scarcely 200 miles (321.86 kilometers) wide in some places, the Andes chain is the longest in the world. It stretches over four thousand miles (6,437.2 kilometers) along the continent's west coast. This range also boasts some of the earth's tallest peaks. Only Asia's Himalaya Mountains are higher than Mount Aconcagua, which frowns down on western Argentina.

Over three-fourths of South America lies in the tropics. The Andes, however, have a climate all their own. Low down, where they break out of the eastern flatlands, the air is hot and tropical plants can grow. Above 7,000 feet (2,133.6 meters) the air becomes cooler. Great forests thrive, giving way at slightly higher altitudes to crop and grazing land. Here the Incas and other Indian peoples built their great civilizations. Beyond, to the frozen snowline, the air grows gradually colder. Above

13,000 feet (3,962.4 meters), only moss, lichens, and tough, grasslike plants, called sedge, survive.

Where Argentina, Bolivia, and Chile meet, the Andes split into two ranges. They are separated by a windswept plateau about 400 miles (643.72 kilometers) wide. This is the Altiplano, as it is called in Spanish, or "high plateau." It is nearly two and a half miles (4.02 kilometers) above sea level and almost perfectly flat—a strange sight nestled between the towering peaks.

Many rivers and streams tumble from the Andes and other highland areas. The great Amazon River begins in the Andes of Peru and flows 3,900 miles (6,276.27 kilometers) to the Atlantic Ocean. The Amazon contains more water than any river on earth—over 4 million cubic feet (113,200 cubic meters) pour into the Atlantic each second! Small ships can sail more than two thousand miles (3,218.6 kilometers) upstream to the foot of the Andes.

Other major rivers include the Mag-

dalena in Colombia, the São Francisco in east Brazil, and the Orinoco, life stream of Venezuela. Another, the Paraguay-Paraná, flows southward through Brazil, Paraguay, and Argentina. In South America, only the Amazon is longer and contains more water.

The Amazon carries water away from a huge plain called the Amazon Basin—an area almost as big as forty-eight of the fifty United States! This basin is one of two major flatlands in South America. Its heat and rainy downpours support hundreds of miles of densely packed trees, making the Amazon the world's largest rain forest.

Quite different from the first plain is the second. It stretches across Paraguay and most of Argentina, and is made up of two distinct areas—the Gran Chaco and the Pampa. The Gran Chaco is a dry region with scrubby trees widely spaced. Farther south and closer to the coast, rainfall supports the Pampa, a nearly treeless grassland ideal for cattle and sheep grazing.

The grassy Pampa gives way in the south to a strip of dry, shrubby land known as Patagonia, which covers most of South America's narrow tail. Only the Atacama Desert, between the Chilean Andes and the Pacific Ocean, is more barren.

Aside from the Andes, South America contains two other upland areas. The Brazilian Highlands separate the Amazon Basin from the Gran Chaco and reach nearly two thousand miles (3,218.6 kilometers) inland from the Atlantic. In places they are quite rugged, with spectacular waterfalls that drop over scenic cliffs. Iguassu Falls is one of the most breathtaking. Waters from its 275 falls crash thunderously over a rocky expanse more than one and a half miles (2.41 kilometers) wide.

Despite the many rivers which empty themselves along South America's 15,000-mile (24,140-kilometer) coastline, the continent has few good natural harbors. Even fewer islands hug its shores. The only large ones are Trinidad and Tobago, off Venezuela, and the Galápagos, west of Ecuador. A lacy string of smaller islands follows the coast of Chile south to Tierra del Fuego. Here the continent ends as the Andes sink their bony slopes into the sea.

Caribbean Sea
TRINIDAD
ATLANTIC OCEAN
Lake Maracaibo
VENEZUELA
Orinoco
GUYANA
Angel Falls
GUIANA HIGHLANDS
SURINAME
COLOMBIA
LLANOS
PAKARAIMA MTS.
FRENCH GUIANA
CORD. OCCIDENTAL
CORD. ORIENTAL
Equator
Negro
Amazon
MARAJO ISLAND
Chimborazo
ECUADOR
Amazon
Cape Sao Roque
A N D E S
Madeira
Mt. Huascaran
PERU
CORD. OCCIDENTAL
B R A Z I L
PACIFIC OCEAN
SERRA DOS PARECIS
Sao Francisco
BRAZILIAN
CORDILLERA ORIENTAL
Lake Titicaca
BOLIVIA
MATO GROSSO PLATEAU
HIGHLANDS
SERRA DO ESPINHAÇO
ATACAMA DESERT
Tocantins
Bandeira Pk.
GRAN CHACO
PARAGUAY
Tropic of Capricorn
Parana
Iguassu Falls
Paraguay
SERRA DO MAR
Mt. Ojos del Salado
CHILE
A N D E S
Parana
Uruguay
Mt. Aconcagua
URUGUAY
ARGENTINA
Rio de la Plata
PAMPA
ATLANTIC OCEAN
PATAGONIA
FALKLAND ISLANDS
Strait of Magellan
TIERRA DEL FUEGO
© Rand McNally & Co.
Cape Horn

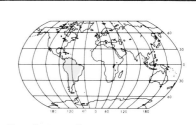

South America Facts

Fourth largest continent
Fifth in population: 263,300,000
25 cities with over 1 million population
Highest mountain: Aconcagua, 22,831 feet (6,959 meters)
World's highest waterfall: Angel Falls, 3,189 feet (972 meters)
Equator passes through

All of the world's natural sodium nitrate is blasted from the Atacama Desert, which stretches 600 miles (965.58 kilometers) along the coast of Chile. Nitrate is used to make fertilizer and explosives.

South America's Amazon River contains more water than the Nile, Yangtze, and Mississippi rivers combined—or nearly one-fifth of all the fresh water that runs off the earth's surface. Its outpouring is so great that the water of the open sea is fresh for over 200 miles (321.86 kilometers) beyond the river's mouth.

63

South America/
Countries and Cities

Roads
Railroads

South America is but one name for a continent which today is divided into twelve independent nations. Along with its Central American and Mexican neighbors, South America is often called Latin America.

Most South Americans speak either Spanish or Portuguese—tongues based on the language of ancient Rome, or *Latium*. Europeans brought these Latin languages with them when they conquered the continent in the mid-1500s. Spanish is the official language of all but three of the continent's twelve nations. Portuguese is spoken in Brazil, South America's largest and most populated country.

Brazil spreads over half the continent and is one of the world's biggest nations. Only the Soviet Union, China, Canada, and the United States are larger in area. Over 134 million people live in Brazil, more than in all other South American countries combined.

Brazil is a nation on the go. São Paulo, to the south, is the major industrial city of the continent. Factories are going up in ever-increasing numbers, particularly in the coastal region between São Paulo and Rio de Janeiro.

Two small nations just north of Brazil also have official languages other than Spanish. The Dutch-speaking people of Suriname and the English-speaking people of Guyana have ancestors who were mainly Hindustanis—people from India—or black Africans. These groups were brought to South America by the Dutch and English during colonial days

High in the Andes near Cuzco, Peru, lie the ruins of Machu Picchu—once a walled Incan city. Unknown to the Spanish, it may have been a last hideaway for the doomed Inca people.

to work on sugar plantations along the marshy coast.

Sixty-six percent of the people in neighboring French Guiana are black or of mixed African and European ancestry. French is the official language, for French Guiana really belongs to faraway France. In years past, French Guiana was famous for its prison colony on Devils Island, and for the dreaded prison camps at Kourou and Saint-Laurent on the mainland. These camps were closed in 1945.

Spanish-speaking Argentina, to the far south, differs greatly from these three small pockets of northern settlement. After Brazil, Argentina is the largest South American nation in both area and population. The country sprawls over 1,068,301 square miles (2,766,889 square kilometers) and contains over 30 million people. Its lifeblood is the Pampa, a huge plain where rich soil supports fields of grain and where lush grass feeds great herds of cattle.

Argentina has attracted large numbers of Europeans. Its capital, Buenos Aires, has mushroomed until the population of the city and its suburbs tilts past ten and a half million.

Argentina is especially powerful among the nations of the southern part of the continent. These include Chile, whose nearly 12 million people live in the narrow strip of land between the Pacific and the Andes, and Uruguay and Paraguay, tiny countries with fewer than three and a half million citizens apiece.

The more northern countries of Peru, Ecuador, and Bolivia have much in common, for their Andean plateaus and valleys once belonged to the golden empire of the Incas. The Incas ruled over a highly civilized realm of about 3 million subjects. Today, Peru alone has about 9 million Indian citizens—more than any other country in the Western Hemisphere. Many Indians still speak Quechua—the language of the ancient Incas.

Cuzco, in modern-day Peru, was the capital of the empire. Still standing is the fortress which crowned the ancient city.

Its walls consist of such massive boulders that scientists cannot understand how the Incas were able to build with them.

Farther north along the Pacific coast is Colombia, gateway to the continent. Only through Colombia can land travelers reach Central America. Bogotá, Colombia's capital and largest city, was among the first settled in the New World.

For years neighboring Venezuela was one of South America's poorest nations. But all this changed when, in 1917, vast oil deposits were discovered at Maracaibo. Today, Venezuela has the highest standard of living in South America. And, Venezuela and Ecuador are Latin America's only members of the powerful Organization of Petroleum Exporting Countries (OPEC).

But whatever their power, location, or size, the countries of South America are linked by the strong Latin character of their continent. This tie sets them apart from the people of any other single continent.

Chile possesses a wealth of minerals. It mines about 16 percent of the world's copper and vast amounts of iron ore, nitrates, and coal.

Brazil's capital is the ultra-modern city of Brasília, built in 1960 in the central uplands.

South America / Life on the Land

Close to half the people of South America make their living by farming. Most farms are quite small and can often barely produce enough food—mostly corn and beans—to feed the families that own them. Most of the farmers use old-fashioned ways of farming, with no machinery.

However, there are many huge, modern farms and ranches owned by wealthy people. These farms, some of which are larger than many of the states of the United States, grow immense crops of coffee, wheat, sugar, bananas, and other foods, most of which are sold

eighth largest producer of oil. Several South American countries are also major suppliers of emeralds, silver, and gold.

There are a number of large, modern cities, and more and more factories are being built. Cloth and processed foods such as canned meats, flour, and refined sugar are the chief products of the factories. However, South America is far behind Europe and North America in manufacturing.

Life in the big cities of South America is much like life in the cities of North America or Europe. There are tall,

Over 400 years ago, the great Inca empire thrived in South America. Legend has it that the first Incas, Manco Capac and his sister, were created by the sun god on the Isle of the Sun in Lake Titicaca.

Soccer is the national sport of several South American countries. It is played by both amateurs and professionals.

Weaving is an age-old art in the Andes, one passed down from generation to generation. Indian women spin thick Alpaca wool into yarn to make warm ponchos, hats, and other clothing.

or traded to other parts of the world. Much of the world's coffee is grown in South America, especially in Brazil. Argentina exports large amounts of wheat to other parts of the world.

Herds of sheep and beef cattle are also raised on giant ranches. Argentina is the third largest producer of beef in the world and exports more beef than any other nation. It is also the fourth largest wool producer in the world.

South America is rich in many minerals. Much of the world's tin and copper come from South American mines. The little country of Venezuela is the world's

modern buildings, airports, and busy streets. Many city dwellers have radios, television sets, and other conveniences. But elsewhere, people usually live in old-fashioned ways, in tiny villages where there are only dirt roads and no electicity. Many of the Indian people of Peru, Bolivia, and Ecuador still live almost exactly as their ancestors did during the time of the Inca Empire, four hundred years ago. And in the steamy Amazon forest, many small tribes of Indians still live by hunting and primitive farming, as they have done for thousands of years.

Oil Exported

Oil Fields

Coffee Bean
Farming

Fishing

Emerald Mining

Mining

Shipping

Agricultural Area

The Amazon

Rubber

Brazil Nuts
Harvested

Cotton

Spanish-style
Architecture

Indians of Peru

Mahogany
Logging

Agricultural Area

Machu Picchu
(Inca Ruins)

Fishing in
Lake Titicaca

Soccer

Brasilia

Mining

Anchovy Fishing

Mining

Rio de Janeiro

Light Industry

Trees Tapped
for Tannin

Coffee Grown

Copper

Agricultural Area

Cattle Raising

Beef for Export

Fishing

Wheatlands

Bonito Fishing

Lumbering
and Sawmills

Sheep Herding

67

South America/Its Animals

Vast tropical forests spread over much of South America and are the home of a great number of creatures. The big, spotted cats called jaguars prowl among the trees by night, and herds of little piglike peccaries root in the underbrush. One kind of large, hoglike tapir lives here. It is related to both the horse and rhinoceros, and its nose ends in a short trunk.

Many creatures live up in the trees. Little, long-legged sloths, hanging upside down from branches, inch themselves slowly along as they feed on leaves. Monkeys of many kinds shriek, howl, whistle, and chatter from the treetops—red uakaris, that look like sad old men; long-tailed, black-furred woolly monkeys; large-eyed douroucoulis; and golden marmosets.

Brightly colored parrots, macaws, toucans, and other birds flash from tree to tree.

In the rivers swim caimans, the alligators of South America, and many fish including the vicious, flesh-eating piranha, with its razor-sharp teeth. A school of piranhas can devour an animal down to the bare bones in a matter of minutes! Anacondas, giant snakes often more than thirty feet (9.14 meters) long, lurk in some rivers, waiting to seize unwary animals that come to the shores to drink.

On the plains of South America live bushy-furred giant anteaters, which may be more than six feet (1.82 meters) long from tip of nose to end of tail. Here, too, are found long-legged maned wolves, which have been described as

looking like a fox walking on stilts.

Many animals live in the long range of mountains along the west coast. This is where the humpless camels of South America are mostly found—llamas, alpacas, guanacos, and vicuñas—small, heavily furred beasts that live in herds. The spectacled bear roams the mountain slopes. It gets its name from the circles of yellowish fur, like eyeglass frames, around its eyes. The chinchilla, a bushy-tailed, mouselike creature with the finest, silkiest fur in the world, lives high up on the snow-capped heights. And gliding through the air between mountain peaks is the great South American condor with a wingspread of nearly ten feet (3.04 meters). It is a kind of vulture that feeds on the bodies of dead animals.

Nearly a fourth of all the world's animals live in South America. Because forests are rapidly being cleared, and plains used for farming and grazing, many of these animals are in serious danger of becoming extinct.

The mysterious Galápagos Islands lie about 600 miles (965.58 kilometers) off the coast of Ecuador. Here live rare cormorants that cannot fly, great lizardlike iguanas, and giant turtles weighing over 500 pounds (226.8 kilograms).

Sloth

Tapir

Manatee

Scarlet Ibis

Coatimundi

Ocelot

Piranha

Green Turtle

Toucan

Caiman

Spectacled Bear

Llama

Spider Monkey

Red Brocket Deer

Anaconda

Vampire Bat

Chinchilla

Capybara

Jaguar

Howling Monkey

Macaw

Vicuña

Great Anteater

Condor

Guanaco

Maned Wolf

Brazilian Lapwing

Alpaca

Pampas Deer

Blue Marlin

Torrent Duck

Rhea

Elephant Seal

Magellan Goose

Magellan Penguin

Cavy

Black-necked Swan

Sperm Whale

69

In many ways the terrain of most of North America is like that of South America. There is a mass of high mountains in the west, a block of lower highlands in the east, and a huge plain in between.

The western mountains are made up of two main chains that stretch from the arctic shores of Alaska to Panama in Central America. Best known are the Rocky Mountains which rise out of the Great Plains like an enormous blue wall. They are breathtaking in Colorado, where more than fifty peaks soar higher than 14,000 feet (4,267.2 meters).

The Rockies reach northward into Canada, where Mount Robson thrusts upward to 12,972 feet (3,953.86 meters). Here the scenery is wilder than it is in the United States. Evergreen forests cover the mountains' lower slopes. Above timberline—where trees are unable to grow—awesome glaciers crunch their way down stony canyons.

Many separate mountain ranges rise west of the Rockies—the Coast Mountains of Canada, and the Cascades, Sierra Nevada, and Coast ranges of the United States. Inactive volcanoes lie, like sleeping giants, among them. Mount Lassen last moved its mighty shoulders in 1914. Mounts Rainier and ancient Mazama whose hollow core holds the mirrorlike waters of Crater Lake have been dormant far longer. Then in March 1980 Mount St. Helens in Washington, dormant since 1857, erupted with a roar, sending plumes of steam more than a mile high and dropping ash 50 miles away—a reminder that sleeping giants can awaken at any time.

Between the Pacific mountain ranges and the Rockies, in the United States, lies the Great Basin. The Sierra Nevada and the Cascades prevent most of the rain clouds that form over the Pacific from reaching the Great Basin. The dry

A great plain spreads across Canada's Prairie Provinces—Alberta, Manitoba, and Saskatchewan. Saskatchewan wheat ripens in the sun.

A shallow prehistoric sea once covered what was to become Arizona's Grand Canyon. Over millions of years rock layers built up with the rising and falling waters. It took millions more years for the Colorado River to gouge out the canyon.

Mexico's famous Mounts Popocatepetl and Iztaccihuatl can be seen for miles throughout the surrounding countryside. "Popo" is one of America's highest peaks. It is only 2,433 feet (741.57 meters) less than Alaska's Mount McKinley.

southern end of this area is called the Mojave Desert. A desertlike region covers much of the American Southwest and reaches deep into the Mexican state of Sonora.

Mexico also has two main mountain ranges. The Sierra Madre Occidental is in the west and the Sierra Madre Oriental is in the east. Plateau country spreads out between them and it is here that most of Mexico's people live.

Two of North America's well-known volcanoes are in Mexico. They sit side by side in the central region—Popocatepetl, or "Popo" as the Mexicans fondly call it, and Iztaccihuatl. Some people see in Popocatepetl a warrior guarding a beautiful sleeping lady, as the second volcano appears to be. The legends are romantic, but the volcanoes have a fiery past. Iztaccihuatl last erupted in 1868. Popocatepetl has not erupted since 1702, but from time to time it still gives off a puff of smoke—a reminder of the power that lies deep within its boiling core.

Central America, farther south, is mountain country, except for the narrow plains along its coasts. It fairly bristles with volcanoes. There are more than thirty alone in the tiny country of Guatemala.

The uplands on the eastern side of North America are much lower than those in the West, but they have their own charm. In Canada are the Laurentian Mountains. These formed at the edge of a gigantic horseshoe shaped plateau that surrounded Hudson Bay during the Ice Age.

In the eastern United States the largest upland area is the Appalachian chain which reaches from Maine to Alabama. These are old mountains, worn by time and weather. Among them are the White, Green, Blue Ridge, and Great Smoky Mountains.

One of the world's largest plains, the Great Plains, lies in the center of the continent. The land is wonderfully fertile. In eastern Canada farmlands surround Toronto for 150 miles (241.39 kilometers). In western Canada, fields of wheat spread to the horizons. In the United States, the Great Plains form the nation's breadbasket—its wheat-growing lands.

The waters of the Great Plains are carried away by one of the biggest river systems in the world—the Mississippi-Missouri.

The largest freshwater lake in the world is found on the North American continent. Lake Superior, one of the five Great Lakes, was born during the Ice Age when the glacier scooped out the lake beds.

North America reaches beyond the Arctic Circle in the north. The end of the Boothia Peninsula is the northernmost mainland point. At its southern tip, beyond Panama, it dips to within 700 miles (1,126.51 kilometers) of the equator and joins South America.

North America/Countries and Cities

Canada's houses of Parliament, in Ottawa, stand strangely alone amid winter snow and ice. It is here that 386 members of Parliament meet to govern the country's ten provinces and two territories.

Of all the continents, the boundaries between countries are the simplest in North America. Most of the continent is divided among three nations: Canada, the United States, and Mexico.

Borders between countries are never decided upon easily, and such was the case with those in North America. The boundary between Canada and the United States was settled upon in 1783, following the Revolutionary War, and by treaties in 1818, 1842, and 1846. Today, relations between the two countries are close and friendly. The frontier between them is the longest undefended border in the world, 5,525 miles (8,891.38 kilometers).

The boundary between the United States and Mexico was agreed upon only after the bitter Mexican War of 1846 to 1848, and by treaties and purchases of land.

The United States is the giant among the three countries. It has less land than Canada, but has more than nine times as many people. And it has more than three times the population of Mexico. With its vast stores of raw materials and its industrial know-how, enormous quantities of goods—cars, steel, food, and clothing—pour out of the industrial northeast to the country itself and to the rest of the world.

When the Americans revolted against British rule in 1775, the Canadians remained loyal to the crown. Today, they recognize Queen Elizabeth II as official head of state. Nevertheless, Canada is self-ruling. Although a member of the British Commonwealth of Nations, it has its own parliament and prime minister. Canada, too, is rich in natural resources. It is one of the most prosperous countries in the world.

The way of life of people in Canada and the United States is very much alike. Quite different is the way of life in Mexico.

Mexicans can trace their beginnings back to both the highly developed Indian civilizations, such as the Mayas and the Toltecs, and to the Spanish conquerors. Memories of the Indian peoples who ruled the land before the arrival of the Spanish remain alive in such splendid ruins as Teotihuacán, near Mexico City, which contains remarkable pyramids. Links to Spain are present in the country's many churches and palaces, which are like those of sixteenth century Spain. Customs in Mexico, especially in the cities, are in many ways like those of Spain.

Of all the Spanish-speaking countries, Mexico has the most people—more than Argentina, Chile, and Colombia combined—many more than Spain itself. It carries much weight among the Spanish-speaking nations of the world. Important deposits of oil have been found in Mexico in recent years. With oil scarce and expensive, Mexico's future looks highly promising.

Central America covers an area less than a third the size of Mexico. It is made up of six small republics, the Panama Canal Zone (now part of Panama), and newly independent Belize. Here too, the people's roots are Indian and Spanish. For example, the Indian people of Guatemala are descended from the once-mighty Mayan tribes whose ruined cities still rise in eerie splendor out of the jungles of the north. Indian customs are common in Guatemala. On the other hand, the people of Costa Rica have many Spanish as well as Indian ancestors and customs can still be traced to the way of life in Spain.

Panama is cut through by the American-built canal, a waterway with an impressive series of locks and dams. It joins the Atlantic and Pacific Oceans, separated only by the twenty-seven miles (43.45 kilometers) of the slim isthmus.

Greenland, the largest island in the world, is considered part of North America. So are the islands of the Caribbean, sometimes called the West Indies. These sunny islands have a colorful past, and stories still are told of

Mexicans shoot off showers of fireworks and hold gay fiestas to celebrate Independence Day, September 16. Mexico declared its independence from Spain in 1810.

Spanish galleons loaded with silver and gold, and of French and British pirates.

English is the main language of North America, spoken by most Americans and Canadians. About a quarter of Canada's people speak French. Spanish and Indian tongues are spoken in Mexico. Spanish, English, French, Dutch, and several other languages are spoken in the West Indies.

European explorers who visited North America once called it the New World. It was indeed "new" to them. In some ways it still is new—or at least young. Cities which thrived before the arrival of Columbus have disappeared. Today North American cities are all more or less like those of Europe. All have come into being only since the year 1500.

North America/Life on the Land

Ice hockey is a popular sport played by both amateurs and professionals in Canada and the United States. The game began in Canada in 1855 and is that country's national sport.

The United States and Canada, two of the three main nations of North America, are industrial giants. The United States ranks first and Canada is tenth among all the nations of the world in industrial might. North America is rich in forests and minerals, from which many things can be made, and many Canadian and U.S. cities are giant manufacturing centers. The United States produces one-fourth of all automobiles made in the world and one-eighth of all the steel. It is a leading producer of cloth, paper products, natural gas, oil, and many other things. Canada is the main producer of the paper newspapers are printed on and of a number of important metals.

The industry of Mexico, the third main North American nation, is growing. Its main products are clothing and chemicals, with processed foods, rubber products, cement, and fertilizers also important. Some steel is made, and Mexico produces a small number of automobiles. Its main export is cotton. It is also an important oil-producing country.

Canada and the United States are also farming giants. The United States produces about half of all the corn grown in the world as well as a fourth of all the oats. Canada grows much of the world's barley and wheat. Farming is done with modern machinery, and so much extra food is grown that the United States and Canada sell a lot of it to other parts of the world. Large amounts of cattle, hogs, and poultry are also raised, and Canada's fishing fleet helps keep it among the world's leading producers of seafood.

Agriculture is also important in Mexico. The richest farmlands are in the south-central part of the country where the climate is mild and there is plenty of rainfall. The main crop is corn, all of which is grown to feed the Mexican people themselves. Cotton, coffee, sugarcane, and wheat are also raised.

The smaller countries of North America, including Central America and the West Indies, grow important crops of coffee, sugarcane, and bananas. Tobacco is also a main crop in many of the islands of the West Indies. But the main "industry" for some of these islands is to provide fun and relaxation for the many tourists who visit them, especially in winter.

According to folklore, the giant Paul Bunyan and his enormous blue ox Babe created much of America's landscape. They supposedly dug the St. Lawrence River in just three weeks using a scoop shovel as large as a house.

The famous Ballet Folklorico of Mexico performs many dances based on Mexican history and legend. The dancers below wear costumes modeled after those worn by the ancient Mayas, an Indian people who lived in Mexico a thousand years ago.

Mining

Alaskan Pipeline

Oil Fields

Salmon Fishing and Canning

Totem Pole

Lumbering

Fur Trapping

Ski Trails

Canadian Wheatlands

Lumbering

Fishing

Greenland

Canneries

Agricultural Area

Giant Redwoods

Wheat

Potatoes

Mt. Rushmore

Dairyland

Statue of Liberty

Truck Farming

Hollywood

Soybeans

Agricultural Area

Cars Manufactured

Washington, D.C.

Offshore Oil Drilling

Citrus Groves

Longhorn Cattle

Corn

Peanuts

Tobacco

Agricultural Area

Corn

Longhorn Cattle

Cotton

Citrus Groves

Cape Canaveral

Sugarcane

Olmec Sculpture

Oil Fields

Oil Fields

Ruins of Ancient Pyramids

Agricultural Area

Sugarcane Made into Molasses

Coffee

Bananas

North America/Its Animals

North America once teemed with wildlife. But, in just the last hundred years or so, many kinds of creatures have grown fewer, and some are extinct. However, in national parks, and in deserts and other places where there are few people, many kinds of animals can still be found. And some animals have adapted to living near people and busy communities.

The most "typical" North American animal, the big, shaggy buffalo, or American bison, was once nearly wiped out by hunters. But a few were saved, and today herds of thousands still rumble over the rolling plains in a few national parks.

In the northern woods beavers build dams in streams where black bears catch fish. Porcupines amble through the underbrush, and the lynx stalks its prey. Moose, wapiti, and caribou are found in the north, and far in the north tiny herds of long-haired musk-ox wander.

Packs of wolves still hunt in Canada and the northern United States, but their numbers are growing fewer. However, the smart, bold coyote is growing in numbers, and even prowls the outskirts of towns and cities. Flying squirrels, which only come out at night to glide from tree to tree, and also raccoons and squirrels can be found in almost any wooded area. There are rabbits and chipmunks in every meadow.

Twenty-nine kinds of rattlesnakes live throughout North America. Biggest of them is the eastern diamondback, often seven feet long (2.13 meters). The brightly colored and deadly coral snake lives in deserts in the southwest, together with the poisonous lizard called the Gila monster, and poisonous scorpions with as many as a dozen eyes!

Alligators lurk in swamps and rivers of the southeast. Here, too, live big, hulking alligator snapping turtles that lure fish into their mouths by wiggling a tongue that looks like a fat worm. Another southern animal, found as far south as Central America, is the shelled armadillo which rolls itself up into an armored ball for protection.

A few hundred grizzly bears still roam in the northwest, and that is also where the bald eagle, national bird of the United States, soars in the sky. But both these creatures are in danger of becoming extinct.

Sea otters live in the sea on the west coast. And in a bay on the west coast, thousands of some of the biggest of all animals gather each year to mate—California gray whales, which may be as much as forty feet (12.19 meters) long.

Animals live, thrive, and become extinct. They are known only from their fossil remains. The passenger pigeon, however, was seen and painted by John James Audubon, the great naturalist, in 1840.

Apatosaurus
135 Million Years Ago

Tyrannosaurus
70 Million Years Ago

Woolly Mammoth
10 Thousand Years Ago

Great Auk
Mid Nineteenth Century

Saber-Toothed Cat
1 Million Years Ago

Passenger Pigeon
Late Nineteenth Century

Grizzly Bear

Walrus

Herring Gull

Canada Goose

Polar Bear

Mountain Goat

Red Fox

Gray Wolf

Rock Ptarmigan

Bald Eagle

Beaver

Porcupine

Mountain Lion

Moose

Robin

King Salmon

Pronghorn

Elk

Gray Squirrel

Raccoon

White-tailed Deer

Sea Otter

Bison

Cottontail

Willet

Gambel's Quail

Diamondback Rattlesnake

Opossum

Turkey

Peccary

Alligator

California Sea Lions

Armadillo

Roseate Spoonbill

Brown Pelican

Squirrel Monkey

Gray Whale

77

Australia, New Zealand, Oceania/Terrain

The vast expanse of the Pacific is dotted with islands. Some are the tips of volcanoes that push up through the blue waters. Others are atolls, rings of coral surrounding calm lagoons which remain where volcanic peaks have sunk back into the sea. This area includes New Zealand and Australia and is called Oceania.

Australia is the smallest of the continents, yet it has unique features that are world famous—among them the Great Barrier Reef and the "Outback."

The Great Barrier Reef borders the eastern edge of Cape York Peninsula in the north and continues south along the coast for 1,250 miles (2,011.62 kilometers). Coral formations in shades of pink, green, orange, yellow, and purple rise from the ocean floor. Great numbers of different kinds of fish and other sea creatures glide through the tropical waters.

West of the Great Dividing Range, in the central part of the country, is one of the world's lonely desert regions. Australians call it the Outback. Part of it is bush country, where an occasional stunted tree or bush grows. The rest consists of three main deserts—the

Australia, New Zealand, Oceania Facts

Australia
Smallest continent
Population: 15,565,000
Highest mountain: Kosciusko, 7,310 feet (2,228 meters)

New Zealand
Two main islands, North Island and South Island
Population: 3,155,000

Oceania (not including Australia and New Zealand)
20,000 islands—more or less—scattered throughout the Pacific
Population: 5,480,000

The mountains of New Zealand's North Island give way in the southwest to hills and then to raised beaches washed by the sea.

Two of Fiji's 800 islands in the South Pacific are large, with lovely tree-lined beaches. Most of the others are merely piles of sand on coral reefs.

Ayers Rock towers 1,100 feet (335.28 meters) above the flat Australian desert.

Great Sandy, the Gibson, and the Great Victoria. Glaring sun fries the sand, rocks, and clay, and only those animals who have adapted over long centuries to desert life are able to survive.

Rain is kept out of the Outback by the Great Dividing Range. Air moving inland from the Tasman Sea is blocked and forced upward. As it rises it cools and drops its moisture along the coast. The continent's main agricultural area is here. Lush wheat fields and big herds of fluffy-backed sheep have made Australia a leading exporter of grain and wool.

The Great Dividing Range, Australia's main mountain chain, hugs the eastern and southeastern coast for about two thousand miles (3,218.6 kilometers). In the south it dips into the sea and pushes upward again 130 miles (209.20 kilometers) from the mainland to form the island state of Tasmania. The hump-shaped mountains of the Great Dividing Range are old, hammered by the wind and rain for hundreds of millions of years. They are not as spectacular as the Alps or Rockies, yet they have their own haunting beauty, especially in the deep canyons of the Blue Mountains near Sydney.

The southwestern coast also has low mountains, the Darling Range, which prevent the movement inland of rain clouds. The coastal area is fertile, and wheat and sheep are raised here.

Very different from the arid Outback and the agricultural regions around the eastern and southwestern edges of the continent is Cape York Peninsula in the north. Heat and rain combine here to make ideal conditions for the growth of tropical jungles.

New Zealand is often linked with Australia. But they are individual countries separated by nearly 1,200 miles (1,931.16 kilometers) of lonely ocean, and their landscapes are completely different.

Two main islands make up New Zealand. They are appropriately called North and South Island. Snowy mountains jab upward from almost all of South Island and from much of North Island. On the southwest coast of South Island the mountains send long shoulders into the sea where they form waterways as beautiful as the fjords of Norway.

The most unusual area of New Zealand is the volcanic region around Lake Taupo on North Island. Here there are boiling springs, geysers with hot water leaping skyward, strange pools of steaming mud, and tiny lakes with beds of brightly colored rocks. Beautiful waterfalls tumble from the encircling volcanic peaks.

South Island, the larger of the two, has magnificent mountain scenery. Glistening glaciers nestle among the heights, and seventeen peaks soar above 10,000 feet (3,048 meters).

The islands of Oceania are thought of in three parts. Most of Polynesia is east of the International Date Line and includes Hawaii, Samoa, Tahiti, and Easter Island. Micronesia in the central Pacific includes the Marshall, Caroline, and Gilbert islands. Melanesia in the southwest includes the Fiji Islands and New Guinea. New Guinea is the second largest island in the world. Only Greenland is bigger.

An expedition headed by Ferdinand Magellan was the first to sail around the world, 1519 to 1522. Crossing the Pacific, Magellan sighted only two islands and finally landed on Guam. There are thousands of islands in Oceania. To have missed all but two was, in a way, a remarkable coincidence!

Australia, New Zealand, Oceania/Countries and Cities

Roads
Railroads

Darwin

NORTHERN TERRITORY

Cairns

Townsville

QUEENSLAND

Tropic of Capricorn   Alice Springs

AUSTRALIA

WESTERN AUSTRALIA

SOUTH AUSTRALIA

Brisbane

Kalgoorlie

Broken Hill

NEW SOUTH WALES

Newcastle

Sydney

Perth

Adelaide

Canberra
AUSTL. CAP. TER.

VICTORIA

Melbourne

© Rand McNally & Co.

TASMANIA

Hobart

The lands "down under"—that's what Australia and New Zealand are often called. The name grew out of the idea that these lands were directly opposite, under the feet of, Europeans.

In some ways things in the two countries actually are the opposite of those in the Northern Hemisphere. To go north is to head for the warmth of the equator, and to go south is to travel toward cold weather. Winter occurs in July and summer in January. However, only the physical setting is "opposite." Many customs would be familiar to a traveler from Europe or America, for they were handed down by British settlers.

Both countries are members of the British Commonwealth of Nations.

They are self-governing, with elected members of their own parliaments.

Once the islands of Oceania were colonies of foreign powers. Since 1962 many have become independent. The eastern half of New Guinea is a nation. So are Nauru, Fiji, Tonga, Western Samoa, and the Solomon Islands.

In a way, East and West have met in the Pacific. The islanders—descended from Asian ancestors—explored the sea and created highly developed civilizations on some of the islands. Hundreds of years later, explorers from the West "discovered" the lands, and colonies soon followed. Today, remains of the ancient island customs exist side by side with the European way of life.

Auckland

NEW ZEALAND

Wellington

Christchurch

Dunedin

© Rand McNally & Co.

Australia, New Zealand, Oceania/
Life on the Land

Lumbering

Rain Forest

Water Sports

Sheep Raising

Lumbering

Water Conservation

Uranium Prospecting

Cattle Raising

Great Barrier Reef

Aborigines in the Outback

Agricultural Area

Mining

Sheep Raising

Ayers Rock

Rugby

Going to School by Radio

Mining

Opals Mined

Sydney Opera House

Lifeguard Teams

Minerals Mined

Citrus Groves

Agricultural Area

Agricultural Area

Wheatlands

Water Sports

Freighter

Minerals Exported

Fishing

Fruit Grown

Maori Carving

Sheep Raising

More than half of all Australians live in large, modern cities on the coast. Many of these people work in factories and in industry, for Australia is a highly industrialized nation. It produces steel, automobiles, textiles, and machinery.

Many Australians live in the small towns on the outer edge of the Outback, in the areas where there is plenty of grass for raising sheep and cattle. Australia is the world's leading sheepraising country, and in fact, there are about eleven times more sheep in Australia than there are people!

A lot of Australians are farmers who live in the eastern and southern parts of the continent where there is plenty of rainfall. The main crop is wheat, with about two-thirds of all the wheat grown being sold to other countries.

New Zealand is not as industrialized as Australia, although a good deal of manufacturing is done. The main products are woodworking, electrical, and farming machinery. In New Zealand, too, most of the people live and work in or near cities.

However, dairy farming is really the most important part of New Zealand's economy. Sheep and cattle raising follow close behind. New Zealanders eat more meat and butter than people anywhere else in the world with enough left over to sell, in enormous amounts, to other countries.

The people of both Australia and New Zealand live and act very much like people of the United States and Great Britain. Most of them have television sets, automobiles, and other conveniences. Their standard of living is very high.

Australia, New Zealand, Oceania/Its Animals

Many of the animals of Australia are very different from those in other places, for Australia was separated from all other parts of the world for about 50 million years and its animals developed in a different way. Most Australian mammals—the furry, warmblooded animals—are *marsupials*. Marsupials are animals like the kangaroo whose babies are kept in a pouch on the mother's body until they are old enough to care for themselves. Two of the strangest Australian animals are the echidna, or spiny anteater, and the duck-billed platypus. They are furry and warm-blooded mammals, but their babies hatch out of eggs, like birds or reptiles! These two creatures may be much like the first kinds of mammals, many millons of years ago.

Much of Australia is covered by a desert or by dry plains, but many animals live in these dry lands. Kangaroos live in little herds on the plains, where there is grass for them to eat. They are large animals, as much as seven feet (2.13 meters) tall, but there are also "midget" kangaroos, called wallabies.

Another plains marsupial is the wombat, which looks a bit like a beaver without a tail. An expert digger, it makes long tunnels beneath cliffs and boulders in which it sleeps by day. It comes out at night to feed on grass and roots. The bandicoot, also a marsupial, lives in much the same way as the wombat, but eats mostly insects.

One plains dweller is not a marsupial. It is a kind of wild dog known as a dingo that roams the wild areas of the country in packs. However, dingoes are not true natives of Australia. They were brought here thousands of years ago by prehistoric people.

Other desert dwellers are lizards such as the spiny moloch, many kinds of poisonous snakes, and a highly unusual bird known as the emu. The emu cannot fly, stands five and a half feet (1.67 meters) tall, and can run at speeds up to thirty miles (48.27 kilometers) an hour.

In the eastern part of Australia, where there are eucalyptus trees, lives the koala. It looks like a teddy bear, but it isn't the least bit related to any bear, for it, too, is a marsupial that carries its baby in a pouch. Later, when the baby is bigger the mother carries it on her back. Koalas are tree dwellers.

There are many rabbits in Australia, but like dingoes, they aren't natives either. They were brought from England.

On some islands near New Zealand live little reptiles called tuataras. They are the descendants of reptiles that lived before the dinosaurs—the only creatures of their kind anywhere in the world!

Great numbers of sea creatures drift gracefully among the coral reefs—and in the deeper tropical waters—surrounding the islands of Oceania. A few are frightening. Most are brilliantly colored and startlingly beautiful.

Blue Angelfish

Pacific Sheepshead

Albacore

Ocean Sunfish

Eagle Ray

Imperial Angelfish

Regal Angelfish

Sea Horse

Viperfish

Opah

Black Marlin

Triggerfish

Butterfly Fish

Cockatoo

Cassowary

Dingo

Death Adder

Tree Kangaroo

Echidna

Emu

Frilled Lizard

Rabbit

Rock Wallaby

Wombat

Great Gray Kangaroo

Koala

Kookaburra

Red Kangaroo

Platypus

Wandering Albatross

White Shark

Slender-billed Shearwater

Black Swan

The koala looks like a soft, cuddly teddy bear. Small, it weighs less than eighteen pounds (8.16 kilograms) when grown. For six months the cub rides in the mother's pouch. Later it rides on her back, even when she climbs high into the eucalyptus trees for the buds and leaves which are the koala's only food.

Dovey Petrel

Kiwi

Tuatara

Kea

Antarctica

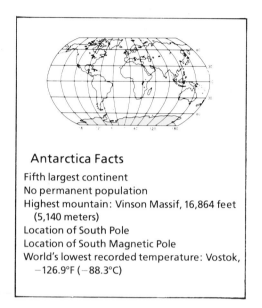

Antarctica Facts

Fifth largest continent
No permanent population
Highest mountain: Vinson Massif, 16,864 feet
  (5,140 meters)
Location of South Pole
Location of South Magnetic Pole
World's lowest recorded temperature: Vostok,
  −126.9°F (−88.3°C)

Antarctica, the coldest continent on earth, rests squarely on the South Pole. It is so cold here that an unprotected visitor would freeze in minutes. In midwinter, June, temperatures inland may drop below −100°F (−73°C).

Because of the tilt of the earth's axis and its path around the sun, Antarctica is without sunlight for months at a time. Even in "summer," the sun's rays strike at such a slanted angle the land receives very little heat.

Most of Antarctica is covered with snow heaped so thick it forms a mile-high plateau at the pole. Bitter winds shriek over the seemingly endless white sheet at speeds averaging forty-four miles (seventy-one kilometers) an hour. In many places the snow has been tightly packed by its own great weight and frozen by the cold to become a massive ice pack. This ice is so heavy it has pressed parts of the land well below sea level. If the ice cap melted, all that

could be seen above the waters would be the craggy peaks of the mountain chain which twists some 3,000 miles (4,827 kilometers) across the continent.

Antarctica covers nearly as much area as Europe and Australia combined. Yet it has no permanent settlements, just small, scientific research stations.

Only 600 miles (965.58 kilometers) separate Antarctica from the tip of South America. But it is so far off the trade routes that explorers did not sight its shores until 1820. More than twenty years passed before Britain's James Ross and his crew sailed through the treacherous ice pack surrounding the continent to find the Ross Sea—a wide gouge in Antarctica's western shore. A wall of solid ice—later to be called the Ross Ice Shelf—prevented their further movement. But they had opened up a route for later overland expeditions.

In 1911, what almost amounted to a race to reach the South Pole occurred. A Norwegian, Roald Amundsen, and four companions achieved their goal on December 14. The Englishman, Robert Scott, and four companions arrived at

Since the continent was discovered in 1820, many nations have sent teams to Antarctica. Dog sleds are still used, but motorized toboggans are more common.

the pole a month later but did not survive the return to their base camp. However, Scott and his men left their contribution to the world's knowledge, too. They collected thirty-five pounds of leaf fossils and several pieces of coal from the frozen earth. From these and more recent finds of reptile bones we know that Antarctica was not always a snow-bound continent. About 200 million years ago it was connected to southern Africa, South America, Australia, and India. Large forests grew in warm swamps, insects darted about, and reptiles roamed the leafy byways.

Today, many warm-blooded animals thrive in the waters on the fringes of the continent. Among these are seals, many types of birds, and the great blue whales. Antarctica's largest land animal, however, is a wingless insect related to the housefly. It is less than one-tenth inch (2.54 millimeters) long.

Halfway between land and sea animals are Antarctica's penguins. These appealing creatures stand upright and resemble little men in tuxedos. Though penguins are birds, they cannot fly. Their wings have become stiff paddles that help them move easily underwater.

Surprisingly, Antarctica's waters hold more marine life than oceans in warmer parts of the globe—about three times the quantity caught by all the world's fishing fleets. Antarctica's frozen land has yielded small amounts of gold, iron, uranium, and coal. It is also thought to contain oil and natural gas.

Many nations claim parts of Antarctica. But the Antarctic Treaty of 1959 pledges these nations to wait until 1989 to settle their claims. What will happen after that? No one knows. But Antarctica's future may well be more exciting than its lonely past.

Emperor Penguin

Adélie Penguin

Krill

Crabeater Seal

Weddell Seal

South Pole Discovered by Roald Amundsen (Norway) December 14, 1911

Southern Black-backed Gull

Vinson Massif Highest Mountain

South Pole

Vostok World's Lowest Recorded Temperature

Fulmar

Cape Pigeon

Ross Ice Shelf

Arctic Tern

Ross Sea

Leopard Seal

Great Skua

South Magnetic Pole

Blue Whale

Tooth Fish

Other Kinds of Maps

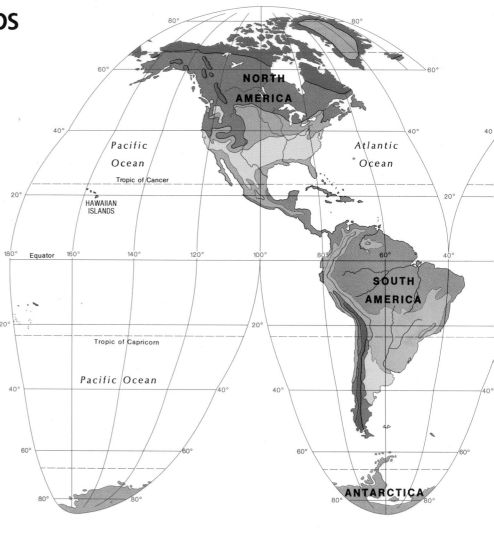

Seasonal Temperatures of the World

Always cold	Hot summer and cool winter
Cold winter and cool summer	Hot summer and mild winter
Cool or cold winter and mild summer	Always hot
Hot summer and cold winter	Always mild

Temperature Chart

Hot = above 20°C (68°F)

Mild = 10°- 20°C (50°- 68°F)

Cool = 0°- 10°C (32°- 50°F)

Cold = below 0°C (32°F)

Scale

0   1000   2000   3000 Kilometers

0   1000   2000 Miles

© Rand Mᶜ Nally & Co.

Colors on a map usually mean something. The legend that accompanies the map explains the meaning of the colors. In the map above, colors show the hot, warm, and cold areas of the earth. At a glance it is possible to understand that the climates of northern South America, central Africa, and southern Asia are alike—always hot. It's also possible to see that southern Australia—south of the equator—has a climate like that of part of North America—north of the equator. Anyone who wonders what "hot" or "cool" means can find that information in the

legend, too. The mapmaker has given a range of temperature readings for those words.

Maps of the world, or parts of it, come in many shapes. For centuries mapmakers have been trying to flatten out the round earth for their maps, which they call *projections*. But no matter how they "peel" its surface, parts of the earth stretch and become distorted.

Gerhardus Mercator tried, in the sixteenth century. He developed a map known as the Mercator Projection. It consists of squares and rectangles

formed by the parallels and meridians. Land areas on this map are greatly distorted near the poles. But this kind of map is still used today by navigators. That's possible because all straight lines are lines of true direction; following them leads to the place the sailor wishes to reach.

In our own century, J. Paul Goode carved up the earth's surface in a new way. In his projection the parallels are straight, but the meridians curve according to certain mathematical rules. Both land and sea areas are accurate on this kind of map.

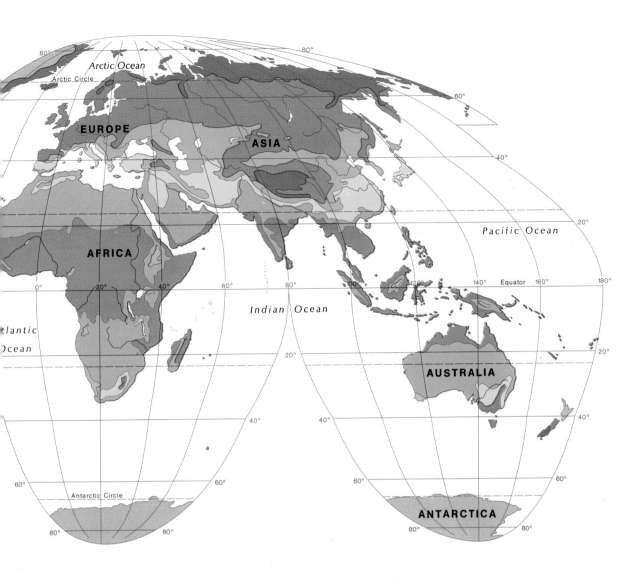

The strips into which the earth is divided give Goode's Projection quite a different look from earlier maps of the earth. The parallels are straight, but the meridians curve inward at the poles. Both land and sea areas are accurate. Greenland is not only its proper size—smaller than South America—but appears to curve over the top of the world.

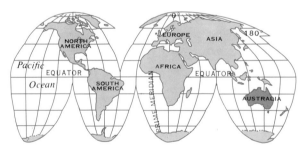

In Mercator's Projection, land areas near the equator are accurate, but those near the poles are greatly oversized. Greenland appears to be larger than South America.

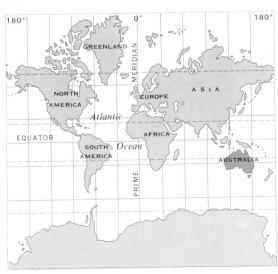

In this polar view, the map looks as though it touches the earth at one point—the North Pole. It is reasonably accurate for a good part of the Northern Hemisphere, but land areas near the equator are badly misshapen. Nevertheless, a polar view is useful, for it shows how close to each other North America, Europe, and Asia are at the pole.

Other Kinds of Maps

Land Use of the World

Manufacturing and trade

Farming and stock raising
for a market

Farming, herding, forestry, hunting,
and fishing for family needs

Forestry for a market

Fishing for a market

Little or no activity

Scale
0   1000   2000   3000   Kilometers
0   1000   2000   Miles

© Rand McNally & Co.

Also in our own century, in recent years, Arthur Robinson arranged the surface of the earth in still another way. His is a modern form of the oval projections known nearly two hundred years ago. It is flattened at the poles, and lands and oceans in the north and south are not distorted as they are on the Mercator Projection.

The map above is a Robinson Projection. Again, colors have meaning—they show world land use. It is possible to read this map and find out where farming, forestry, manufacturing, or trade are done throughout the world.

In preceding pages, world land use was shown in pictorial maps. They were called Life on the Land.

Maps, each with a legend which helps a reader understand it, can give information of many kinds. Rainfall, population, the location of certain minerals such as gold and silver, ocean currents, wind patterns—all can be shown on maps. But the best use of maps is still what they were first made for: to help people find their way from one place to another anywhere on earth.

Because shapes of the continents strongly resemble shapes on a globe, the Robinson Projection like the one above has many uses. A small view appears on all continental terrain pages in this book, showing each continent in relation to the others.

Those Hard Words

Air mass: a body of air a hundred to a thousand miles across and reaching several miles upward.

Altitude: the height above sea level of the earth's physical features.

Antarctic and Arctic zones: the bitterly cold areas surrounding the South and North poles.

Astrolabe: an instrument used to observe the stars' positions. Used before the invention of the sextant.

Atlas: a collection of maps in a book.

Atmosphere: the entire mass of air surrounding the planet Earth.

Atoll: the ring of coral around an ocean lagoon, all that remains after a volcanic island sinks into the sea.

Axis: an imaginary line between the poles. The earth turns around its axis every twenty-four hours.

Barometer: an instrument that measures the weight of the air. Used in weather forecasting.

Barren: any land area that lacks normal vegetation.

Basin: any land area drained by a river and its tributaries.

Beast of burden: an animal used to carry heavy materials or perform other heavy work.

Bush country: a large land area with little vegetation, usually thinly settled.

Butte: an isolated upraised land area with steep sides and a small top.

Canal: any artificial waterway.

Canyon: a deep valley with steep sides.

Cape: a point of land jutting out into water.

Cartographer: a mapmaker.

Chronometer: an instrument used by navigators for measuring time — east-west distances from the prime meridian.

Cirrus: a white wispy cloud formed at very high altitudes.

Coastal: land at the edge of the ocean or sea.

Compass: an instrument for telling direction. A magnetic needle turns freely on a pivot and points to the magnetic north.

Continent: one of the great named divisions of land on earth.

Continental shelf: a shallow undersea area bordering a continent, ending in a steep slope to the deeper ocean.

Contour line: a line on a map joining the land points having the same elevation, or height.

Coral reef: a rocklike deposit of animal skeletons just below the ocean surface. Reefs can be miles long.

Cumulus: a huge summer cloud with a flat base and high fluffy top.

Cyclone: a storm or system of winds spinning around a center of low atmospheric pressure.

Desert: dry land which supports only widely scattered plant and animal life.

Doldrums: an area of calm winds and warm updrafts near the equator.

Downdraft: a downward movement of air, as during a thunderstorm.

Earthquake: a shaking of the earth caused by volcanic or plate action.

Earth scientist: a person who studies the earth or any of its parts.

Earth's crust: the outer layers of the earth.

Earth tremor: a quivering on the surface of the earth.

Easterly: wind blowing from the east.

Elevation: the height to which earth features reach above sea level.

Equator: an imaginary line on globes and maps halfway between the poles.

Erosion: the wearing away or destruction of land by wind, water, and ice.

Export: send a product to another country.

Extinct: no longer existing.

Eye of a storm: nearly calm center of a storm.

Fall line: a line along which rivers plunge from plateaus and hills to the plain below.

Fault: a fracture in the earth's crust.

Feature: an important, usually very noticeable, part of the earth.

Fertile: able to bear fruit or vegetables in great quantities.

Fjord: an ice-carved inlet of the sea between steep cliffs.

Frontal zone: an area of severe weather where two great air masses—one cold and one hot—collide.

Funnel: the funnel-shaped downward section of a storm cloud, particularly in a tornado.

Game preserve: an area where wild animals are protected.

Geologist: a scientist who studies the earth's outer layers.

Geyser: a natural spring that spouts hot water and steam.

Glacier: a large body of ice moving slowly down over an area of land.

Gravitational pull: that force which pulls objects toward itself.

Grid: a set of lines crossing each other on which maps are drawn.

Gulf: part of an ocean or sea reaching into a land area.

Habitat: the place where a plant or animal naturally lives and grows.

Headland: a point of high land jutting out into a body of water.

Hemisphere: half of the earth.

Hill: an upland area of gentle slopes and a broad summit, generally lower than a mountain.

Horse latitudes: about 30° north and 30° south. Areas of descending air and high pressures.

Hurricane: a tropical cyclone with winds of at least seventy-four miles (119.08 kilometers) per hour and heavy rain.

Ice cap: a cover of permanent ice and snow on the earth's surface. For example, Greenland.

Intermontane: between the mountains.

Island: land, smaller than a continent, surrounded by water.

Isthmus: a narrow strip of land joining two larger land areas.

Jungle: a mass of tropical plant growth.

Lagoon: a shallow pond near a larger body of water.

Landform: a feature of the earth's surface.

Landmark: an outstanding feature of the land used as a guide.

Landmass: a large area of land.

Latitude: the distance between parallels, north or south of the equator.

Lava: melted rock which flows out of the earth's surface.

Legend: key to the symbols and colors used on maps.

Longitude: the east-west distance between meridians.

Marine: having to do with the sea.

Marsupials: mammals whose young develop within pouches on the females' abdomens, such as kangaroos and opossums.

Mattang: stick chart used by Micronesian islanders 2,000 years ago to show ocean wave patterns.

Meridians: imaginary lines joining the North and South poles. The distance between meridians is called longitude.

Mesa: an isolated tableland with steeply sloping sides and a large flat land area on top.

Meteorologist: a scientist who studies the earth's atmosphere and forecasts the weather.

Microscopic: invisible to the naked eye unless magnified through a microscope.

Migrate: to move from one region or climate to another in order to survive.

Molten rock: rock turned into liquid by intense heat.

Monsoon: a seasonal wind in southern Asia.

Mountain: a landmass, with steep slopes and a sharp peak, reaching high above the surrounding land.

Natural barrier: any geographical feature which separates two areas.

Navigation: the science of moving around on—or above—the earth.

Nimbus: a dark rain cloud reaching as far as one can see.

Ocean: the whole body of saltwater covering nearly three-fourths of the earth's surface.

Oceanographer: a scientist who studies the sea and everything in it.

Outback: bush country and deserts, found in Australia.

Ozone: a special form of oxygen. High in the atmosphere, a layer of ozone surrounds the earth, screening out the sun's harmful rays. Closer to the earth's surface, ozone sometimes forms as the result of pollution. Even in small amounts, ozone is irritating to breathe.

Pampa: a grass-covered plain found in South America.

Parallels: imaginary lines circling the earth in an east-west direction. Like railroad tracks, they never meet. The distance between parallels is called latitude.

Peninsula: an area of land almost surrounded by water.

Physical: that which can be seen and measured and, perhaps, weighed. Things that have height and width and depth. A physical map shows the earth's major features — mountains, hills, plains, oceans, rivers, lakes.

Piedmont: the area lying or formed at the base of mountains. May consist of plateaus or low hills.

Plain: an area of level-to-rolling, almost treeless land.

Plankton: microscopic animal and plant life found in the sea.

Plateau: large level land area raised sharply above the surrounding land.

Plates: sections underlying the surface of the earth. Their movement may cause faults or other changes in the surface.

Polar: having to do with the North or South poles or the areas around them.

Portolan charts: detailed maps used for navigation by European sailors in the 1500s.

Prehistoric: the time before history was written down.

Prime meridian: the meridian chosen to be 0° or prime meridian. It passes through Greenwich, England.

Quake: to quiver or shake. A shortened term for earthquake. A tremor.

Rain forest: a densely grown tropical woodland with almost daily rainfall. Near the equator.

Range: a series of mountains in a group.

Rapid: part of a river where the current is fast and the surface is broken by large rocks.

Ridge: a long narrow upper crest. Can be of very high formations on mountains, hills, waves, even parts of the ocean floor.

Rift: a deep crack in the earth's crust.

Scale: a mathematical key which tells how much the earth or an area of the earth was reduced to fit on a map.

Sea: a saltwater body smaller than an ocean.

Sea level: the average level of the ocean between high tide and low tide. Land areas are measured above or below sea level.

Sedge: tufted marsh plants.

Seismologist: a scientist who studies earthquakes.

Silt: water-carried earth material, finer than sand.

Smog: a combination of fog and smoke.

Solar energy: power from the sun.

Solar system: the sun and the planets and other space objects which revolve around it.

Space orbit: a circular path outside the solar system.

Spillway: a passage for extra water to run over or around something that stands in its way.

Steppe: a vast level or rolling tract of treeless land in Europe and northern Asia.

Stratus: a wide flat cloud at a low altitude.

Subcontinent: a large peninsulalike area of land. For example, India.

Tectonic: having to do with changes in the shape of the earth's surface and the forces that produce those changes.

Terrain: the landscape.

Tornado: a destructive whirling cyclone over a land area.

Trade winds: the winds that blow out of the horse latitudes toward the doldrums. In the Northern Hemisphere they are the northeast trade winds; in the Southern Hemisphere they are the southeast trade winds.

Trench: a long, narrow, steep-sided ditch in the ocean floor.

Tropics: the area on both sides of the equator where temperatures are always high and rainfall is plentiful.

Tundra: a treeless plain in arctic regions. Areas below the surface are permanently frozen.

Updraft: an upward movement of air.

Upland: high land — mountains, hills, plateaus, mesas, buttes.

Valley: a low area between ranges of hills or mountains.

Volcanic cone: the top of a volcano.

Volcano: an opening in the earth's surface from which molten rock and steam erupt.

Volcanologist: a scientist who studies volcanoes.

Westerly: wind blowing from the west.

Index

plankton, 21
plat, meaning of, 10
plateaus, 10*
  African, 11
  Arabian, 11
  erosion of, 11
  formation of, 10
  intermontane (intermountain),
    10*, 11
  piedmont, 11
  Swiss, 11
Pluto (planet), 6*, 7
  spacecraft and, 7*
Poland, 45*
  manufacturing in, 43
Polaris (star), 19
  mapmaking and, 15
  navigation and, 14
pollution, 25*
Polo, Marco, 60*
Polynesia, 79
Popocatepetl (volcano), 71, 71*
portolan charts, 17*
precipitation
  air masses and, 23
  cycle of, 24
prime meridian, 17
projections, of maps, 86, 87*, 88,
  89*
Prudhoe Bay, Alaskan pipeline
  and, 28*
Ptolemy, Claudius, and
  mapmaking, 15
Pygmies, 50
Pyrenees Mountains, animals in,
  45

Quechua (language), 65
Queen Elizabeth II, Canadian
  head of state, 72

rain, cycle of. See precipitation.
rain forest, 33*, 62
Rainier, Mount, 70
Red Sea, 46*
Republic of South Africa
  climate of, 49
  political control of, 49
  population of, 49
Revolutionary War, boundary
  dispute and, 72
Rhine River, 39
Rhodesia, political control of,
  34*, 49
rice
  China and, 27
  and diet, 26
  planting of, 27
"Ring of Fire," 9
Rio de Janeiro, Brazil, 64
Robinson, Arthur (Robinson's
  Projection), 88, 89*
Robson, Mount, elevation of, 70
Rocky Mountains, 8, 10*, 70
  formation of, 9
Romance languages, 41
Roman Empire, 41*
Rome, Italy, 40
Ross, James, 84
Ross Ice Shelf, 84

Ross Sea, 84
Royal Observatory (Greenwich),
  17
Ruhr Valley, industry in, 39
Rus (tribe), 13
Russia. See also Soviet Union.
  naming of, 13
Russian Steppes, 10
Ruwenzori Range, 46

Sahara Desert, 48
  animals of, 52
"sailing the parallel," 15, 15*,
  16
St. Helens, Mount, 70
Saint-Laurent, 65
St. Lawrence River, 74*
  exploration of, 35*
Samoa, 79
São Francisco River, 62
São Paulo, Brazil, 64
Saskatchewan, Canada, 70*
Saturn (planet)
  composition of, 6*
  temperature of, 6*
Saudi Arabia, 46*, 54
scale, of maps, 19
Scotland, formation of mountains
  of, 8
Scott, Robert, 84, 85
Scottish Highlands, 38, 39*
Sears' Tower, 27*
seismologist, study of earth and,
  36*
Semitic language, 49
shading, mapmaking and, 18
shipping, ocean, 30
Siberia, 54, 56, 57
Sierra Madre Occidental, 71
Sierra Madre Oriental, 71
Sierra Nevada, 70
Sinai Peninsula, 47*
sisal, 50
skyscraper, first, 27
Slavic languages, 41
smog, 25*
solar energy, 6, 29, 29*
solar system, 6*
Solomon Islands, 80
sonar devices, detection of fish
  and, 30
south, meaning of, 7
South Africa, 48
  agriculture of, 50
  Kalahari Desert, 50
  livestock raising in, 50
  manufacturing in, 50
  minerals of, 50
  mining, 50
  mountains of, 46
  republic of. See Republic of
    South Africa.
South America
  animal map, 68
  country map, 64
  life on the land map, 66
  terrain map, 62
South America
  agriculture of, 65, 66
  animals of, 68

climate of, 62
coastline of, 62
desert of, 62
formation of continent of, 8
Inca civilization in, 62
industry of, 66
language of, 64
largest lake in, 62*
minerals of, 66
mining in, 66
mountains of, 62
plains of, 62
prison camps in, 65
rivers of, 62
soccer and, 66*
standard of living in, 66
Southeast Asia
  climate of, 55
  industry of, 58
  rice growing in, 58
  rivers of, 55
  rubber production in, 58
South Island (New Zealand), 79
South Pacific, islands of, 78*
South Pole, 84
  meridians and, 16*
  Roald Amundsen and, 84
  Robert Scott and, 84
Southwest Asia
  agriculture of, 58
  industry of, 58
  oil in, 58
Soviet Union
  coal production in, 57
  desert in, 54
  industry of, 43, 58
  mountains of, 39
  steel production and, 27
space colonies, 7*
spacecraft, launching of, 7*
Spain
  olive growing in, 43
  plateau of, 11
  wine-making industry of, 43
speed of light, 6
spillways, 39
Sri Lanka, 57
steel
  composition of, 27
  producers of, 27
storms, development of, 23
Sumatra, animals of, 60
sun
  earth and, 6
  energy from, 28
  heat of, 6
Superior, Lake, 71
Suriname, language of, 64
Sweden, 45
Swiss Plateau, 11

Tahiti, 79
Tanganyika, Lake, 49
Tanzania, 48*, 49
Tasmania, 79
Tasman Sea, 79
Taupo, Lake, 79
Teotihuacán, ruins of, 72
Thailand, 55, 57
Tibet

altitude of, 10
animals of, 60
Indus River and, 54
plateau of, 10, 54
Tierra del Fuego, 62
timberline, 70
Titicaca, Lake, 62*, 66*
Tobago, 62
Tokyo, Japan, population of, 32
Toltec civilization, 72
Tonga, 80
tornadoes, 23*
trenches, ocean. See ocean
  trenches.
Trinidad, 62
Trondheim, Norway, founding of,
  40
Tunisia, 46, 48
Turkey
  agriculture of, 57
  plateau of, 11
  population of, 57

Uganda, 49
United Nations Trust Territory
  (UNTT), 34*
United States
  agriculture of, 71, 74
  industry of, 72, 74
  language of, 35*
  mountains of, 71
  Panama Canal Zone and, 72
  plateaus of, 11
  political boundaries of, 35
  standard of living of, 72
  steel production and, 27
Ural Mountains, 39, 54
Uranus (planet), composition of,
  6*
Uruguay, population of, 65

Valdez, Alaska pipeline and port
  of, 28
Venezuela
  oil and, 65, 66
  Organization of Petroleum
    Exporting Countries (OPEC)
    and, 65
  river of, 62
  standard of living of, 65
Venus (planet), 7
  spacecraft and, 7*
  temperature of, 6*
Vespucci, Amerigo, 12*
  naming of America and, 13
Victoria, Lake, 46, 46*, 49
Victoria Falls, 46*
Vietnam, meaning of, 56
Vikings
  Canada and, 13
  Cape Cod and, 13
  Newfoundland and, 13
  North America and, 13
  Russia and, 13
Virginia (state), naming of, 13
volcanoes, 9, 9*, 78
  active, 70
  Aleutian Islands and, 20*
  eruption of, 9*
  extinct, 21

Credits:
Cover Illustration: George Armstrong

Illustrations:
Rod Ruth, page 8 (lower), all Animal Maps and accompanying illustrations (pages 44–45, 52–53, 60–61, 68–69, 76–77, 82–83), Antarctica Map (page 85).
Tom Dunnington, all Life on the Land Maps and accompanying illustrations (pages 42–43, 50–51, 58–59, 66–67, 74–75, 81).
George Armstrong, 9, 12 (upper, middle), 13, 14, 15 (lower), 21 (upper). James Conahan, 15 (upper), 21 (lower), 22 (lower), 25. David Cunningham, 26, 28–29. JoAnn Daley, 6, 7. Sharon Elzaurdia, 29 (upper), 33. Larry Fredericks, 30–31. Herbert Gotsch, 34, 35. Robert Russo, 10 (upper), 16 (lower), 22 (upper), 23 (upper). Gene Sharp, 10–11 (lower), 18, 19 (lower), 27, 35, 36–37. Werner Willis, 19 (upper).

Photographs:
Aerial Fotobank, 19. American Museum of Natural History, 27. Mark Antman/Stock, Boston, Inc., 29 (upper left). Bayerisches Armeemuseum Ingelstadt by J. Correggio, 34. Bruno Barbey/Magnum Photos, 49 (lower), 63 (lower). Albert Bendelius/Van Cleve Photography, 84. Borowicz/Alpha, 63 (upper), 65 (right). Jules Bucher/Photo Researchers, Inc., 26. D'eca/Free Lance Photographers Guild, 65 (left). Dick Dietrich/Free Lance Photographers Guild, 71 (upper). R.G. Everts/Photo Researchers, Inc., 41. Courtesy, Field Museum of Natural History, Chicago, 14 (lower). FPG/Alpha, 29 (right). Esther A. Gerling/Alpha, 71 (lower). Malcom J. Gilson/Free Lance Photographers Guild, 39 (upper left). S. Glatter/Alpha, 56. L. Goldman/Alpha, 54 (right). Hara/Alpha, 39 (upper right). Jean Heilbrunn/Free Lance Photographers Guild, 33 (right). J. Alex Langley/DPI, 25. Lazi/Free Lance Photographers Guild, 46. Lustig/Alpha, 47. Malak/Alpha, 72. Malak/Free Lance Photographers Guild, 70. Milt and Joan Mann, 29 (lower). Merrifield/Free Lance Photographers Guild, 33 (left). James G. Moore, U.S. Geological Survey, 9. Josef Muench/Alpha, 54 (left). NASA, 17 (lower), 24. National Maritime Museum, London, 14 (upper). The Newberry Library, Chicago, 12, 17 (upper). Eberhard E. Otto/Alpha, 39 (lower left). Pastner/Alpha, 48, 49 (upper). Paul Petroff/Free Lance Photographers Guild, 73. G.R. Roberts; Nelson, New Zealand, 78. H. Armstrong Roberts, 9 (inset), 32. G.R. Russell/Free Lance Photographers Guild, 64. Jerry Stransky/Webb Photos, 11 (lower). Wide World Photos, 23. Hamilton Wright/Free Lance Photographers* Guild, 62.

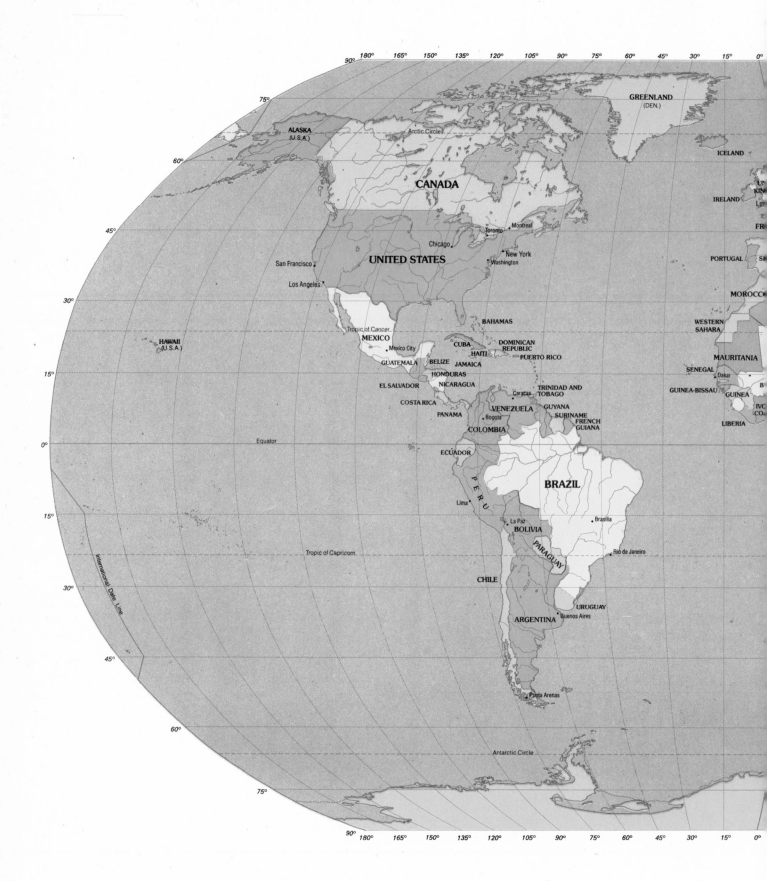

90° 180° 165° 150° 135° 120° 105° 90° 75° 60° 45° 30° 15° 0°

75°

GREENLAND
(DEN.)

ICELAND

60° Arctic Circle

ALASKA
(U.S.A.)

IRELAND UN
KIN
Lo

CANADA

45° Montreal
Toronto

Chicago

FR

New York
UNITED STATES Washington

San Francisco PORTUGAL S

30° MOROCCO

Los Angeles

Tropic of Cancer WESTERN
BAHAMAS SAHARA

HAWAII MEXICO
(U.S.A.) Mexico City CUBA DOMINICAN
REPUBLIC MAURITANIA
HAITI
GUATEMALA BELIZE JAMAICA PUERTO RICO SENEGAL
15° HONDURAS Dakar B
EL SALVADOR NICARAGUA TRINIDAD AND GUINEA-BISSAU GUINEA
TOBAGO IVC
COSTA RICA Caracas CO
VENEZUELA GUYANA LIBERIA
PANAMA SURINAME
Bogota FRENCH
COLOMBIA GUIANA

0° Equator

ECUADOR

P BRAZIL
E
R
U

15° Lima
La Paz Brasilia
BOLIVIA

Tropic of Capricorn PARAGUAY

Rio de Janeiro

CHILE

30° URUGUAY
Buenos Aires
ARGENTINA

International Date Line

45°

Punta Arenas

60°

Antarctic Circle

75°

90° 180° 165° 150° 135° 120° 105° 90° 75° 60° 45° 30° 15° 0°